UNIVERSITY LIBRARY
UW - STEVENS POIN

1980s Project Studies/Council on Foreign Relatio

STUDIES AVAILABLE

THE MIDDLE EAST IN THE COMING DECADE:
From Wellhead to Well-being?
Studies by John Waterbury and Ragaei El Mallakh

REDUCING GLOBAL INEQUITIES
Studies by W. Howard Wriggins and Gunnar Adler-Karlsson

RICH AND POOR NATIONS IN THE WORLD ECONOMY
Studies by Albert Fishlow, Carlos F. Díaz-Alejandro, Richard R. Fagen, and Roger D. Hansen

CONTROLLING FUTURE ARMS TRADE
Studies by Anne Hessing Cahn and Joseph J. Kruzel, by Peter M. Dawkins, and by Jacques Huntzinger

DIVERSITY AND DEVELOPMENT IN SOUTHEAST ASIA:
The Coming Decade
Studies by Guy J. Pauker, Frank H. Golay, and Cynthia H. Enloe

NUCLEAR WEAPONS AND WORLD POLITICS:
Alternatives for the Future
Studies by David C. Gompert, Michael Mandelbaum, Richard L. Garwin and John H. Barton

CHINA'S FUTURE:
Foreign Policy and Economic Development in the Post-Mao Era
Studies by Allen S. Whiting and by Robert F. Dernberger

ALTERNATIVES TO MONETARY DISORDER
Studies by Fred Hirsch and Michael W. Doyle and by Edward L. Morse

NUCLEAR PROLIFERATION:

Motivations, Capabilities, and Strategies for Control

Studies by Ted Greenwood and by Harold A. Feiveson and Theodore B. Taylor

INTERNATIONAL DISASTER RELIEF:

Toward a Responsive System

Stephen Green

STUDIES FORTHCOMING

The 1980s Project will comprise about 30 volumes. Most will contain independent but related studies concerning issues of potentially great importance in the next decade and beyond, such as resource management, human rights, population studies, and relations between the developing and developed societies, among many others. Additionally, a number of volumes will be devoted to particular regions of the world, concentrating especially on political and economic development trends outside the industrialized West.

The Middle East in the Coming Decade

The Middle East in the Coming Decade

FROM WELLHEAD TO WELL-BEING?

JOHN WATERBURY

RAGAEI EL MALLAKH

Introduction by Catherine Gwin

1980s Project/Council on Foreign Relations

McGRAW-HILL BOOK COMPANY
New York   St. Louis   San Francisco
Auckland   Bogotá   Düsseldorf   Johannesburg   London   Madrid
Mexico   Montreal   New Delhi   Panama   Paris   São Paulo
Singapore   Sydney   Tokyo   Toronto

Copyright © 1978 by the Council on Foreign Relations, Inc. All rights reserved. Printed in the United States of America. No part of this publication may be produced, stored in a retrieval system, or transmitted, in any form or by any means, electronic, mechanical, photocopying, recording, or otherwise, without the prior written permission of the publisher.

The Council on Foreign Relations, Inc. is a nonprofit and nonpartisan organization devoted to promoting improved understanding of international affairs through the free exchange of ideas. Its membership of about 1,700 persons throughout the United States is made up of individuals with special interest and experience in international affairs. The Council has no affiliation with and receives no funding from the United States government.

   The Council publishes the quarterly journal *Foreign Affairs* and, from time to time, books and monographs which in the judgment of the Council's Committee on Studies are responsible treatments of significant international topics worthy of presentation to the public. The 1980s Project is a research effort of the Council; as such, 1980s Project Studies have been similarly reviewed through procedures of the Committee on Studies. As in the case of all Council publications, statements of fact and expressions of opinion contained in 1980s Project Studies are the sole responsibility of their authors.

The editor of this book was Michael Schwarz for the Council on
Foreign Relations. Thomas Quinn and Michael Hennelly were the editors
for McGraw-Hill Book Company. Christopher Simon was the designer and
Teresa Leaden supervised the production. This book was set in
Times Roman by Creative Book Services, Inc.

Printed and bound by R. R. Donnelley & Sons.

Library of Congress Cataloging in Publication Data

Waterbury, John.
The Middle East in the coming decade.

(1980's project/Council on Foreign Relations)
Bibliography: p.
1. Near East—Economic conditions.
I. El Mallakh, Ragaei, joint author.
II. Title. III. Series: Council on Foreign
Relations. 1980s project/Council on Foreign
Relations.
HC407.7.W37   330.9'56   77-26299
ISBN 0-07-068445-6
ISBN 0-07-068446-4 pbk.

1 2 3 4 5 6 7 8 9 R R D R R D 7 8 3 2 1 0 9 8

HC
407.7
.W37
c.2

Contents

317455

317452

Foreword: The 1980s Project

The studies in this volume chart the likely future course of economic and political development in the Middle East. They discuss the ways in which the many states of the region, divided as they are between rich oil producers and others with much more meager resources but with vast and needy populations, may participate in what has come to be called North-South relations—relations between the industrialized and the developing nations—during the next 10 to 20 years. They are part of a stream of studies to be produced in the course of the 1980s Project of the Council on Foreign Relations, each of which analyzes an issue or set of issues likely to be of international concern over the middle-range future.

The ambitious purpose of the 1980s Project is to examine important political and economic problems not only individually but in relationship to one another. Some studies or books produced by the Project will primarily emphasize the interrelationship of issues. In the case of other, more specifically focused studies, a considerable effort has been made to write, review, and criticize them in the context of more general Project work. Each Project study is thus capable of standing on its own; at the same time it has been shaped by a broader perspective.

The 1980s Project had its origins in the widely held recognition that many of the assumptions, policies, and institutions that have characterized international relations during the past 30 years are inadequate to the demands of today and the foreseeable demands of the period between now and 1990 or so. Over the course of the next decade, substantial adaptation of institutions and behavior will be needed to respond to the changed circumstances of the 1980s and beyond. The Project seeks to identify those future conditions and the kinds of adaptation they might require. It is not the Project's purpose to arrive at a single or exclusive set of goals. Nor does it focus upon the foreign policy or national interests of the United States alone. Instead, it seeks to identify goals that are compatible with the perceived interests of most states, despite differences in ideology and in level of economic development.

The published products of the Project are aimed at a broad readership, including policy makers and potential policy makers and those who would influence the policy-making process, but are confined to no single nation or region. The authors of Project studies were therefore asked to remain mindful of interests broader than those of any one society and to take fully into account the likely realities of domestic politics in the principal societies involved. All those who have worked on the Project, however, have tried not to be captives of the status quo; they have sought to question the inevitability of existing patterns of thought and behavior that restrain desirable change and to look for ways in which those patterns might in time be altered or their conse-quences mitigated.

The 1980s Project is at once a series of separate attacks upon a number of urgent and potentially urgent international problems and also a collective effort, involving a substantial number of persons in the United States and abroad, to bring those separate approaches to bear upon one another and to suggest the kinds of choices that might be made among them. The Project involves more than 300 participants. A small central staff and a steering Coordinating Group have worked to define the questions and to assess the compatibility of policy prescriptions. Nearly 100 au-thors, from more than a dozen countries, have been at work on separate studies. Ten working groups of specialists and generalists have been convened to subject the Project's studies to critical scrutiny and help in the process of identifying interrela-tionships among them.

The 1980s Project is the largest single research and studies effort the Council on Foreign Relations has undertaken in its 55-year history, comparable in conception only to a major study of the postwar world, the War and Peace Studies, undertaken by the Council during the Second World War. At that time, the impetus to the effort was the discontinuity caused by worldwide conflict and the visible and inescapable need to rethink, replace, and supplement many of the features of the international system that had prevailed before the war. The discontinuities in today's world are less obvious and, even when occasionally quite visible—as in the abandonment of gold convertibility and fixed monetary parities—only briefly command the spotlight of public attention. That new institutions and patterns of behavior are needed in many areas is widely acknowledged, but the sense of need is less urgent—existing institutions have not for the most part dramatically failed and collapsed. The tendency, therefore, is to make do with outmoded arrangements and to improvise rather than to undertake a basic analysis of the problems that lie before us and of the demands that those problems will place upon all nations.

The 1980s Project is based upon the belief that serious effort and integrated forethought can contribute—indeed, are indispensable—to progress in the next decade toward a more humane, peaceful, productive, and just world. And it rests upon the hope that participants in its deliberations and readers of Project publications—whether or not they agree with an author's point of view—may be helped to think more informedly about the opportunities and the dangers that lie ahead and the consequences of various possible courses of future action.

The 1980s Project has been made possible by generous grants from the Ford Foundation, the Lilly Endowment, the Andrew W. Mellon Foundation, the Rockefeller Foundation, and the German Marshall Fund of the United States. Neither the Council on Foreign Relations nor any of those foundations is responsible for statements of fact and expressions of opinion contained in publications of the 1980s Project; they are the sole responsibility of the individual authors under whose names they appear. But the

Council on Foreign Relations and the staff of the 1980s Project take great pleasure in placing those publications before a wide readership both in the United States and abroad.

Edward L. Morse and Richard H. Ullman

1980s PROJECT WORKING GROUPS

During 1975 and 1976, ten Working Groups met to explore major international issues and to subject initial drafts of 1980s Project studies to critical review. Those who chaired Project Working Groups were:

Cyrus R. Vance, Working Group on Nuclear Weapons and Other Weapons of Mass Destruction

Leslie H. Gelb, Working Group on Armed Conflict

Roger Fisher, Working Group on Transnational Violence and Subversion

Rev. Theodore M. Hesburgh, Working Group on Human Rights

Joseph S. Nye, Jr., Working Group on the Political Economy of North-South Relations

Harold Van B. Cleveland, Working Group on Macroeconomic Policies and International Monetary Relations

Lawrence C. McQuade, Working Group on Principles of International Trade

William Diebold, Jr., Working Group on Multinational Enterprises

Eugene B. Skolnikoff, Working Group on the Environment, the Global Commons, and Economic Growth

Miriam Camps, Working Group on Industrial Policy

1980s PROJECT STAFF

Persons who have held senior professional positions on the staff of the 1980s Project for all or part of its duration are:

Miriam Camps	*Catherine Gwin*
William Diebold, Jr.	*Roger D. Hansen*
Tom J. Farer	*Edward L. Morse*
David C. Gompert	*Richard H. Ullman*

Richard H. Ullman was Director of the 1980s Project from its inception in 1974 until July 1977, when he became Chairman of the Project Coordinating Group. At that time, Edward L. Morse became Executive Director of the Project.

PROJECT COORDINATING GROUP

The Coordinating Group of the 1980s Project had a central advisory role in the work of the Project. Its members as of December 31, 1976, were:

W. Michael Blumenthal   *Bayless Manning*
Richard N. Cooper   *Theodore R. Marmor*
Carlos F. Díaz-Alejandro   *Ali Mazrui*
Richard A. Falk   *Joseph S. Nye, Jr.*
Tom J. Farer   *Michael O'Neill*
Edward K. Hamilton   *Marshall D. Shulman*
Stanley Hoffmann   *Stephen Stamas*
Samuel P. Huntington   *Fritz Stern*
Gordon J. MacDonald   *Allen S. Whiting*
Bruce K. MacLaury

COMMITTEE ON STUDIES

The Committee on Studies of the Board of Directors of the Council on Foreign Relations is the governing body of the 1980s Project. The Committee's members as of December 31, 1976, were:

W. Michael Blumenthal   *Walter J. Levy*
Zbigniew Brzezinski   *Joseph S. Nye, Jr.*
Robert A. Charpie   *Robert V. Roosa*
Richard N. Cooper   *Carroll L. Wilson*
James A. Perkins (Chairman)

The Middle East in the Coming Decade

Introduction: A Region in Transition

Catherine Gwin

In the coming decade, the governments of the Middle East, intent on rapidly modernizing their economies and enhancing state power, will seek to extend the reach of central authority over their growing populations. And, in this period that promises lightning economic growth for some, tensions between nationalism and regionalism will mount. These strains in the consolidation of the state and the construction of regional relations are highlighted in the following studies by John Waterbury and Ragaei El Mallakh as major themes of the next decade's era of transition in the Middle East. For many years, the volatility and tragedy of the Arab-Israeli conflict have diverted attention from the regional drama of emerging nation-states. But both Waterbury and El Mallakh assume that this long-enduring dispute will not be the decisive issue in the 1980s.[1] The central dynamic in the years ahead will be determined instead by how newly amassed

[1]Neither author focuses directly on the Arab-Israeli conflict. Nor does either discuss the political and economic future of Israel in the course of assessing prospects for development in the Middle East. Their treatment of future relations among states in the region suggests that the present solidarity among the more and less conservative Arab states engendered by the Arab cause against Israel will not remain a dominant force for cohesion through the next decade. And further economic development within Israel will not figure significantly in the domestic developments of other states in the region, since full normalization of relations with Israel is unlikely to occur for some time to come.

1

oil wealth is put to use in the transformation of national economies and in the drive for regional power.

The two studies comprise one of five volumes in the 1980s Project that analyze economic and political trends in the various regions of "the South." The authors in each of the regional volumes are concerned with the prospects for sustained economic development in the states of their regions during the next 10 to 15 years; the extent to which regional cooperation will become a major feature of growth and development strategies; and the way in which the states of the different regions, in the pursuit of national objectives, will choose to relate to the industrialized countries of the East and the West. Each volume is designed to stand on its own as a useful projective analysis of a separate region. And each volume fits into the overall effort of the 1980s Project—to analyze and prescribe desirable ways of handling some of the major issues that are likely to be the subject of international contention in the decade of the 1980s and beyond.

The regional survey papers contribute to that effort by assessing the capacities, priorities, and goals of the South that will have a bearing on any attempt to redesign relations between the world's rich and poor nations. Through an exploration of growth and development prospects and policy predispositions in the five regions of the developing world, the papers indicate what sorts of demands the states of the South are likely to make in international economic dealings and how similar or dissimilar will be the evolving interests and needs of the great diversity of developing states. The regional studies also address the question of whether increased regional cooperation will provide the Third World with effective mechanisms for collective self-help and whether such cooperation will help or hinder reform of the international economic order. Finally, they ask if a desirable accommodation between North and South can be accomplished by reform of the international economic system alone or if there are distinct political demands at issue which also require consideration.[2]

[2]The other regional volumes are: Guy J. Pauker, Frank H. Golay, and Cynthia H. Enloe, *Diversity and Development in Southeast Asia*, 1977; and

2

No region of the developing world is likely to have a greater impact on the course of North-South relations in the 1980s than the Middle East. Indeed, the issue of economic development in the South as a whole has gained legitimacy and commanded more eager attention from developed countries in recent years not least because of the demonstrated power of the oil-exporting countries of the Mediterranean and Middle East.

As early as 1971, observers of the world oil industry pointed out that the balance of power among oil-producing and exporting countries and oil-consuming and importing countries was shifting decisively in favor of the producing countries. As noted then:

The winds of change for the oil industry that have been stirring throughout the decades since 1950 have now risen to hurricane proportions. The aim of major oil-producing countries in this vortex is clearly to maximize their governments' "take" out of the value of their oil productions and obtain increasing control over oil operations. To achieve this, these countries—already formally joined in the Organization of Petroleum Exporting Countries since 1960—have now effectively combined to wield the economic and political power of an oil monopoly.[3]

With world oil trade having become a sellers' market, the oil-exporting countries undertook to dictate to the giant oil companies the price of oil, level of royalties and taxes, and terms of nationalization of company property. In 1973, when the Arab oil-exporting countries instituted embargoes and production cut-

---

forthcoming volumes by Riordan Roett and Albert Fishlow on Latin America; by Lloyd and Susanne Rudolph on South Asia; and by I. William Zartman, Colin Legum, and Lynn K. Mytelka on Africa—all published for the Council on Foreign Relations by McGraw-Hill, New York. In addition to these regional studies, the 1980s Project has published two volumes of papers on North-South relations that prescribe ways in which developed and developing countries' interests might be harmonized and the goals of each brought nearer achievement: Albert Fishlow, Carlos F. Díaz-Alejandro, Richard R. Fagen, and Roger D. Hansen, *Rich and Poor Nations in the World Economy*, 1978; and W. Howard Wriggins and Gunnar Adler-Karlsson, *Reducing Global Inequities*, 1978—both published for the Council on Foreign Relations by McGraw-Hill, New York.

[3]Walter J. Levy, "Oil Power," *Foreign Affairs*, vol. 49, July 1971, p. 652.

backs to affect the outcome of their war with Israel, and the Organization of Petroleum Exporting Countries (OPEC) took advantage of the tense political situation to escalate the price of oil, the shift to a new balance of power in the oil industry took on the appearance of a larger turning point in history.

As one seasoned observer of the Middle East has noted, OPEC's quadrupling of oil prices at the end of 1973 was not directly tied to the Arab-Israeli war but was a product of "the feeling that this was the time for the nations of the Middle East to assert themselves and to change the terms of their relations with the West."[4] Although there was some talk in 1973–1974 of the oil-dependent West using economic and military power against the oil-producing states of the Middle East, [5] such actions were never seriously considered. The United States sought, instead, to improve its already good relations with Iran and Saudi Arabia—the two leading producers in OPEC—on whom it counted to maintain security and stability in the Persian Gulf region against any attempt by the Soviet Union or its followers to destabilize the area. And the Western European states and Japan—far more dependent on oil exports from the Middle East than the United States—scrambled to assure exporting countries of their "friendship" in the hope of maintaining secure access to petroleum supplies. Thus, in the few years since the onset of the oil revolution, oil power has demonstrated its ability not just to dictate to private companies but to influence the governments of important powers.

It has also influenced the governments of lesser powers. Emboldened by OPEC's dramatic success in asserting control over the international petroleum market, the less developed countries (LDCs) of the South have pressed forward with a host of demands for change in international economic and political affairs. In so doing, they have looked to OPEC for support in forcing

[4]John C. Campbell, "Oil Power in the Middle East," *Foreign Affairs*, vol. 50, October 1977, p. 97.

[5]See, for example, Robert W. Tucker, "Oil: The Issue of American Intervention," *Commentary*, vol. 59, January 1975, pp. 21–31; idem, "Further Reflections on Oil and Force," ibid., March 1975; letters from readers on these articles, ibid., April 1975, pp. 4–16; author's answers, ibid., pp. 16–21.

concessions on international economic reform from the petroleum import-dependent North—voicing support for the Arab cause against Israel and for OPEC price hikes in exchange for OPEC's involvement in the South's collective bargaining with the North and in the hope of obtaining new funds for development from the oil-rich. In their effort to establish a new world order, the LDCs have also looked on OPEC as an example of the way that groups of underdeveloped but resource-rich states can seize opportunities to increase their nations' wealth and thereby accelerate national economic development.

Despite the euphoria of the LDCs following OPEC's actions in 1973–1974, relations between North and South have not been revolutionized in the wake of the oil industry revolution. "Other OPECs" have not evolved. And, as the study by John Waterbury suggests, OPEC has not shown itself to be an organization dedicated to the creation of a new international economic order. What motivates the member states of OPEC, and what has to date given it operational solidarity, is the assessment that joint action will better serve each member's national interests than will independent, competitive efforts. Moreover, while the oil exporters have established an ability to serve their national economic and political interests by deciding on petroleum prices together, they have provided themselves with the means to exercise far greater independence of action by accumulating enormous new wealth. However, they have not reduced their dependence on the West. They are caught up with the West (including Japan) in an economic relation from which neither can, nor wants to, escape. The West needs secure supplies of oil and cooperation from the states with large petrodollar surpluses in managing the international monetary system. The newly oil-rich states seek industrial and military technology from and investment opportunities in the industrially more advanced West.

The economic interdependence of oil-exporting and oil-importing states is reinforced in the Middle East by political ties. Notwithstanding the enormous arms buildup by the leading oil-exporting states, the global military balance and the relationship of the superpowers remain as relevant as ever to the security of the states in the region. Iran, regardless of its desire to build up the strength and capacity to rely on itself and exercise an independent foreign policy, does not have the power, ultimately, to defend itself against the Soviet Union. And Saudi Arabia, a contender for regional power, will rely heavily for years to come on outside military expertise as well as weapons technology. All governments in the area face the closer threat, moreover, of internal instability and rebellion against grave domestic inequities. From their exposed position in a sea of Southern poverty, Middle East elite groups of both the left and the right seem likely to follow accommodationist positions with the North on the whole host of international economic issues that now comprise the agenda of North-South dialogues.

While the present governments of the oil-rich states will lend some support to the poorer countries of the South in order both to enhance their own international status and to stave off criticism from the non-oil-rich within and outside the region, they are not likely to use oil to lubricate the collective muscle of the South in a way that threatens their continued partnership with the North. A radical change in the governments of the more conservative oil-rich states might give rise to more substantial support for Third World measures of collective self-help, but the prospect of a moderate Middle East position in North-South dealings during the next 10 to 15 years is put forth by both Waterbury and El Mallakh. However, while El Mallakh sees the evolution of relations with the North as a unifying force in the region, bringing states together in efforts at collective bargaining and multilateral undertakings, Waterbury expects attempts by Middle East states to strike nationally advantageous bilateral bargains with states of the North to reinforce other sources of divisiveness in the region. Indeed, Waterbury foresees a decade of intense competition for hegemony in the Maghreb (between Morocco and Algeria), in the Fertile Crescent (between Syria and Iraq), and in the Persian Gulf area (between Iran and Saudi Arabia). This competition will, Waterbury concludes, undermine all attempts at regional integration.

El Mallakh's assessment of the prospects for regional development stands in marked contrast to Waterbury's analysis. Look-

ing with an economist's eye at the abundance of available resources for economic growth—including increasing petro-earnings
and revenues from the reopened Suez Canal—he foresees an era
of relatively smooth economic growth assisted by regional cooperation. A major feature in this era of regional cooperation,
El Mallakh asserts, will be a pattern of good close relations
among Iran, Egypt, and Saudi Arabia. These three countries
have complementary interests deriving from their very different
socioeconomic attributes that, El Mallakh contends, will stimulate joint efforts to bring stability and cohesion to the region
as a whole. Reflected in the two authors' differing assessments
of trends in regional relations are the tensions between nationalism and regionalism, between cohesive economic incentives
and divisive political inclinations, and between self-confident and
defensive policy predispositions that for a long time have troubled
the governments of the Middle East.

In their drive to build viable nation-states, Middle East elites
face a welter of domestic problems that could lead them to follow
narrow nationalistic policies. As economic modernization proceeds, it is reasonable to assume that new socioeconomic tensions within Middle East states will exacerbate long-enduring
communal antagonisms. To date, the social and economic structures of most Middle East countries have precluded the development of political cohesion among economic groups. But the
processes of education, urbanization, and industrialization and
the efforts of ideologically motivated political groups are suc-
ceeding in causing a new definition of issues in terms of rich and
poor, exploiter and worker. The distribution of new oil wealth
exacerbates internal problems that are often rooted in the fact
that groups such as the Kurds in Iran and Iraq find themselves
in state systems that have not allowed them much scope for the
expression of a distinctive communal identity. Although central
governments in most of the Middle East states have become
increasingly strong—buttressed by growing armies, internal security networks, and national revenues—and have for the first
time become focal points of the daily lives of their citizens, some
communal conflicts are likely to prove intractable and the threat
of coups d'état is likely to persist. Where language, religion, and

7

nationality combine to set groups at odds (as in the Sudan or Iraq)[6] armed conflicts or at least a high level of domestic instability will be hard to avoid. To do so will require feats of political prowess by groups of ruling elites who have not yet demonstrated their ability to exercise effective leadership over previously ignored segments of their populations—segments that, in turn, have little reason yet to trust a centralized state authority.

Widening the circle of those who benefit from development represents the opposite side of the coin of expanding central authority. In the Middle East, in contrast to most other parts of the Third World, neither process need be impeded by the shortage of financial resources. But how rapidly segments of each society's population are incorporated into the economy and the polity will not be determined alone by the translation of oil revenues into high rates of economic growth. In the past two decades, throughout the developing world, impressive rates of economic growth and development have in many instances occurred alongside of continuing mass poverty.[7] The persistence of widespread poverty in the face of sustained growth is the result, in part, of the kind of growth strategies that developing countries have followed and that their economic relations with the industrially more advanced countries have fostered. While the Middle East may be alone in the Third World in its opportunity to institute major economic transformation without in any way im-

[6]There is also the very special matter of the Palestinians. In the absence of a settlement of the Arab-Israeli conflict mandating Palestinian statehood, the Palestinians will doubtless remain a source of tension not only for Israel but also in inter-Arab politics. Currently, 1 million Palestinian Arabs on the West Bank and in the Gaza Strip, in addition to nearly 400,000 within the 1967 borders of Israel, live under Israeli control. Palestinians also constitute sizable communities in Jordan, Syria, Lebanon, and Kuwait. Three distinct situations seem plausible for the future: (1) a continuation of Israeli control over a large portion of the Palestinian Arab community; (2) an Arab-Israeli settlement that provides for a Palestinian state on the West Bank and in Gaza; or (3) an Arab-Israeli settlement in which Jordan absorbs most of the Palestinian Arabs. No one of these promises freedom from continuing communal conflict.

[7]For a discussion of the global dimensions of poverty, see the study by Gunnar Adler-Karlsson, "Eliminating Absolute Poverty: An Approach to the Problem," in *Reducing Global Inequities*.

pinging on the high standards of living of its elites, no government has yet been compelled by domestic political pressures to undertake far-reaching reform of existing inequities. Both studies that follow suggest that domestic political pressures for reform are likely to mount. But government expenditures on internal security measures will also increase, especially given the governments' emphases on tight internal security as an underpinning for their international ambitions. Though neither author is, therefore, confident about the prospects for relatively smooth and peaceful development in the region, El Mallakh, a development economist, more than Waterbury, a political analyst, expects that the accumulation of new wealth in the Middle East will induce constructive, broad-based development activities. And he expects that pressures for reform from within will compel the Middle East states to join together to meet the challenges that face them all. In contrast, Waterbury sees growing domestic pressures and the unequal distribution of oil wealth as obstacles to cohesion likely to reinforce other forces of divisiveness that have traditionally set Middle East states at odds with one another.

A radical revolution in any one but the smallest of Middle East states could likely have a destabilizing effect on all parts of the region, especially if such political change were to occur in one of the conservative states that now entertains visions of playing a dominant regional role. Most governments—especially in Iran and Saudi Arabia—are therefore likely to have an interest in supporting some degree of progressive change in neighboring states. It is, in large part, this self-interest in the stability of their neighbors that will lead, in El Mallakh's view, to such regional developments as strong and progressive Saudi-Egyptian-Iranian ties and increased regional development planning. Yet, while Iran and Saudi Arabia may wish to see peaceful development in neighboring states, each wants also, Waterbury argues, to tie its poorer neighbors into dependent relations that bolster its own regional position at the expense of the other emerging regional powers. To the extent that this ambiguity causes animosities within the region, it will work against the additional goal of reducing the influence over intraregional affairs of foreign powers, which usually provide aid to one side or another in any quarrel. It is, in the end, that goal of the Middle Eastern states—to take control over their own affairs—that may generate the resolution of the tension between nationalism and regionalism. But the shape of the resolution is not likely to make itself clear until well into the future.

Multilateral relations among the states in all regions of the Third World are in a period of transition. Existing regional organizations that have been devoted to economic integration have fared poorly, but there is now evidence of a trend toward new forms of regional collaboration. This trend results in part from the developing countries' desire to improve their relative bargaining strength vis-à-vis the industrialized countries of the North on whom they depend for markets, credits, and technology. Regional and subregional caucuses and pacts are among many sorts of collective bargaining units that operate under the same basic idea as does OPEC—that concerted efforts provide increased leverage and inhibit mutually detrimental competitive practices. The continuing Euro-Arab dialogue is an example of an attempt at regional collective bargaining.

Renewed enthusiasm for regional cooperative arrangements derives also from the LDCs' desire to reduce economic dependence on the North. On a regional basis, "collective self-reliance" may take such forms as joint industrial enterprises, regional technology research centers, and schemes to enhance food security through the buildup of regional grain reserves and greater production capabilities. In the Middle East, the use of Arab oil money to fund a regional development bank, cooperative efforts at agricultural development in the Sudan, and various funds for regional development assistance are examples of this new kind of collective self-help.

In addition, there appears to be a growing realization in all parts of the Third World that regional neighbors are becoming increasingly vulnerable to each other's actions—in security as well as in economic affairs. On the one hand, there has been a sizable increase—albeit from a very small base—of intraregional trade and investment over the last five years, while on the other hand, there has been growing concern over the potential for conflict among emerging regional powers. As the willingness of independent states to entrust their national security to foreign powers wanes, as outside powers question the desirability of risking major power confrontations in diverse regional theaters, and as states within Third World regions increase their capacities to contend for regional hegemonic advantage, agreements on a variety of intraregional security procedures—including regional arms limitation agreements, regional pacific settlement procedures, and regional agreements on norms of nonintervention—will take on new importance. While such measures represent the most pressing regional business throughout the Third World, they are probably the least likely sort of activities to make headway on even an ad hoc, informal basis.

The oil revolution that changed relations between petroleum-exporting and petroleum-importing countries filled the coffers and changed the political map of the Middle East. As a result of newly amassed wealth, the potential in the Middle East for economic cooperation to contribute positively to general regional stability seems greater than in any other region of the Third World. Sizable financial resources are available which could be used, if the governments that control them chose to do so, to influence affairs within and between other states. These resources provide, also, the economic wherewithal to sustain the costs of economic integration programs that tend to have long-term payoffs but few and unevenly distributed short-term benefits. In the past, regional integration schemes among developing countries have tended to lead to insufficient gains and outright losses for the industrially least developed member-states. To overcome the inequitable distribution of costs and benefits, mechanisms (preventive, compensatory, and corrective) are needed that ensure the industrially less developed states of special treatment. The success of these mechanisms depends not only on complex collective decision-making procedures but also on considerably greater initial funding than has been made available to LDC integrative schemes in the past.[8] Such undertakings

[8]For a discussion of the problem of unequal gains, see the article by Lynn K. Mytelka, "The Salience of Gains in Third World Integrative Systems," *World Politics*, vol. 25, no. 2, January 1973, pp. 236–250; and her study on the prospects for economic development in Africa, in the forthcoming 1980s Project volume on Africa.

clearly require a greater political commitment to regional integration than has been in evidence to date in the limited free trade area schemes. In the Middle East, where there is such a huge diversity of capabilities among states—some with large financial resources but small labor forces, others with arable land but insufficient financing for agricultural development, and still others with trained workers but too few jobs—regional (as distinguished from national) development would seem to make good economic sense.

In addition, several political motivations exist in the Middle East that could provide a powerful force for cohesion. The first, as noted above, is the interest on the part of the more conservative oil-rich states to support the maintenance of domestic stability in neighboring regimes. Also, given the porosity of borders, population from poor countries may cross over and attempt to settle in richer ones. This may present few problems for sparsely populated Saudi Arabia, but Iran and Kuwait probably cannot long afford for their regional neighbors to continue to be hopelessly poor. The ambition of newly rich petroleum-exporting states, especially Iran, to play an influential regional role may also provide an incentive for enhanced regional cooperation. A further factor contributing to cohesion, important particularly to the behavior of Saudi Arabia, is the vision of pan-Arab unity. Based on a shared linguistic and religious tradition, pan-Arabism has long been an emotionally strong unifying theme that, when focused in an anti-Israeli campaign, has demonstrated the power to bridge a gulf between ideologically hostile regimes such as those in Iraq and Saudi Arabia. Should a settlement come in the Arab-Israeli dispute, the cohesive force of pan-Arabism may well be dissipated, but the desire of Saudi Arabia to be a leader of the wider "Arab nation" is likely to survive as long as does its monarchy. None of these political motivations provide unambiguous support for regional integration, however. Nor do the cultural sources of cohesion generate formulas for overcoming problems of unequal distribution of power in the region.

To emphasize pan-Arabism as a unifying force isolates Iran from the other Islamic states of the region and could well encourage competitive subregionalism rather than cooperative regionalism. Pan-Arabism has radical variants, moreover, that can be fueled by the oil wealth of such countries as Libya and Iraq. If the present regime in Saudi Arabia emphasizes pan-Arab unity, it not only puts itself at odds with Iran but it also runs the risk of losing its leadership position in the Arab world to a less moderate voice. A focus on Islam—the dominant religion in Iran as well as in the Arab states—as a unifying force would include Iran, but the practices of Islam tend to work against modernization. Therefore, modernizing elites in the Middle East may choose not to emphasize their common religious tradition. The inability of the Middle East states to capitalize on these cultural sources of cohesion is reinforced by the huge disparities that exist among states in the region and are described in quite considerable detail by Waterbury.

For the stronger and richer Middle East states, the option of building regional arrangements as frameworks within which to foster regional economic development and stability may compete with aspirations to establish a clear hegemonic position. For to cooperate with one's regional rivals is to constrain oneself. The desire to exercise a more important role on a global scale as well as to exercise maximum policy flexibility in national economic affairs may compete with desires to initiate viable regional economic integration schemes. Indeed, for some of the governments in the richest Middle Eastern states the goal of establishing close relations with countries of the North—who are willing to trade the making of an industrial society for assurances of oil—may divert energies from the building of regional institutions.

The poorer Middle Eastern states—including Egypt, the most populous—are likely to get some increased development support through new regional arrangements, but probably not in the amounts nor in the form they desire. The bulk of development assistance from rich neighbors is likely to flow through bilateral channels—tying the weaker states into new relations of dependency—unless they can, together, press for broader, multilateral development efforts in the region. The differences of opinion expressed in the analyses by Waterbury and El Mallakh delineate the trade-offs involved for both the stronger and the weaker states.

The enormous upsurge in government revenues in the oil-rich states of the Middle East will make it difficult for outside states to exert influence over the course of development there. Many countries no longer need traditional kinds of economic assistance and can be expected to make aid available to the poorer states of the region in their quest for regional power and influence. Consequently, outside threats to withhold economic aid will retain little of their previous effect. Economic costs of withholding coveted technology—civilian or military—will be acceptable neither to Western business executives in competition for burgeoning new markets nor to Western governments concerned about their balance of payments or their influence in the region. The clear need to enlist the cooperative participation of the oil-rich states in international monetary affairs and in the smooth functioning of the petroleum economy will also inhibit Northern governments from putting political pressure on Middle East governments in international forums. States outside the region are, therefore, likely to have little leverage to bring to bear on how Middle East regimes cope with local communal conflicts or internal dissension. Nor will outside powers have much direct influence over domestic policies that affect the nature of income distribution and the meeting of basic needs in the developing Middle Eastern societies.

To the contrary, efforts on the part of the North to engage the petroleum-rich states in international development assistance programs will increase the potential influence of Middle East states on international development strategies and international economic management procedures. The ability of these states to play a prominent role in international affairs is, however, heavily dependent on their ability to achieve stable development at home. All states require a degree of domestic stability as an underpinning for international action. In the case of the richer states of the Middle East, stable progress will also help them assert the independence of foreign policy that they seek and that they require to play a leading role within the group of emerging middle powers. Northern states can assist in this effort by recognizing the political importance of that independence of policy. Also, they can attempt to create a link between progressive development and the international recognition that the leading Middle Eastern states seek. But to do so requires consensus in the North and a foresighted energy policy within and among the Northern states.

What impact outside powers have on the Middle East is more likely to shape events not in but *among* states in the region. Two issues may be worth noting here in particular: the role of outside powers in the buildup of conventional arms in the region and the treatment of emerging regional powers.

In no other region of the developing world is agreement on containing an arms race *less* likely to emerge from arms purchasers within the region and *more* likely to require collaborative efforts on the part of outside arms-trading nations.[9] All of the larger states in the Middle East are engaged in a rapid and awesome expansion of arms and armed forces. Only some of the massive military expenditures can be said to be related to the Arab-Israeli dispute. Iran, not a party to that dispute, has spent huge sums (nearly $12 billion between 1971 and 1976) on the purchase of the most modern and sophisticated weapons available. Though it is not clear for what or against whom these weapons are aimed—surely they are not deterrent or defense against Iran's most powerful political enemy, the Soviet Union— the Shah views Iran's military strength as an attribute of power, and it is his intent to make Iran a military force to be taken into account in the Persian Gulf region and the nearby reaches of the Indian Ocean.[10] Saudi Arabia's military buildup, though not so far advanced as Iran's, is comparable. It is motivated—but only partly—by Saudi Arabia's preoccupation with the Arab-Israeli conflict. Though Saudi Arabia would likely be only marginally involved in the actual military operations of a new war with Israel, Saudi weapons would probably be made available to the

[9]For an extended discussion of possible measures to curb the vast international weapons trade that has grown throughout the world in recent years, see the 1980s Project publication by Anne H. Cahn and Joseph Kruzel, Peter M. Dawkins, and Jacques Huntzinger, *Controlling Future Arms Trade*, published for the Council on Foreign Relations by McGraw-Hill, New York, 1977.

[10]This assessment of the military buildup in the states of the Middle East was informed by Campbell, "Oil Power in the Middle East."

front-line Arab states. In addition, the establishment of a modernized armed force is regarded as a sine qua non of Saudi leadership in the Arab world and as a counterweight to the Iranian military buildup. Large sums are thus being spent on modern weapons and on the expansion of an army and air force that can wage modern war against a range of potential enemies.

In each Middle East country, the armed forces rely on outsiders for weapons, weapons technology, and military expertise. And it appears for now that the foreign ally—whether the United States, the Soviet Union, or others—will not let any client state in the region fall into a dangerously weaker military position. For example, the military buildup in Iran has provoked further arming of Iraq by the Soviet Union and is likely to produce an Arab reaction in which Saudi Arabia, Egypt, and others feel the need for greater unity and strength to oppose Iranian imperialism. Given the competition in the West among arms merchants, combined with the need for the West to remain on good terms with Middle East oil producers and those regimes that pose themselves in opposition to radicalism and communism in the Middle East, it is difficult to see where the inclination to stem the Middle East arms race is to come from. While one could argue that Iran and the Arab states are arming themselves beyond reason, their apparent reasons are more political than they are strategic. Rational arguments to the effect that they are really not buying more security with enormous expenditures in arms, but only increasing the level of destructive capability in the region, are not likely to sway leaders determined to enhance their own and others' perceptions of their nation's position in the world.

It may be that the pace of the military buildup will soon peak in the Middle East simply because few countries other than Saudi Arabia can afford to sustain it and pursue rapid industrialization at the same time. But the arms race will not come to a dead standstill, especially if it is tied to the buildup of industry and new export markets. Joint initiatives on the part of outside powers to slow the transfer of military might would clearly be desirable if they could be accomplished so as to maximize the confidence of states within and outside the region that a balance of power was being maintained among the contending regional parties. But this seems as unlikely as the exercise of restraint on the part of the arms purchasers. What may be important under the difficult circumstances is the ability of the major powers to give recognition to the diffusion of power in the world which has resulted from the oil revolution and occurred in ways that minimize the importance of arms and armed forces and maximize the value of political action. Who speaks on issues of international monetary reform and who mediates local disputes in subregions of the Middle East are not unimportant issues in this regard.

To give recognition to the creation of new power in the world is to recognize, however, that the diffusion of power has been uneven. OPEC has not, for example, led to a generalized new "commodity power" as once predicted.[11] Nor has the Middle East as a unit gained power and influence in the world. Rather, in the Middle East—as in other regions of the developing world—states are emerging as new middle powers that seek to play a predominant regional role and exercise international influence. And it is the policies of these key regional states which are likely to determine, in large part, the position of their regions in the world.

Existing world powers should accord these emerging regional powers the status they seek, particularly in the management of intraregional affairs. There are likely to be costs involved in affording this kind of treatment to emerging middle powers. There are possible costs not only to each major power's own sense of security and fulfillment of interests but also to the needs and interests of weaker states that will feel the power and influence of the dominant regional states. One problem that the creation of new Middle East power centers poses for the interna-

[11]See C. Fred Bergsten, "The Threat from the Third World," *Foreign Policy*, no. 11, Summer 1973, pp. 102–124. Bergsten and others argued in the early 1970s that other commodity cartels would be formed in the wake of the success of OPEC; that they would, like OPEC, come to be able to dictate the terms of production in a number of significant raw material industries; and that, as a result of their ability to control prices and supply flows, they would transfer to the LDCs power and influence in international affairs. While a number of producer associations have in fact been formed, they do not wield the same sort of generalized power and influence now exercised by OPEC.

tional system is how to expand the circle of international economic "managers" without threatening the progress in trade and financial management that has occurred among the industrially advanced countries of the West or without breaking up the international economic system into competing economic blocs. In addition, the ability of multilateral institutions to act in defense of human rights and in support of meeting basic human needs may not be enhanced by the greater participation of newly emergent middle powers sensitive to encroachments on national sovereignty and, therefore, opposed to international programs that intrude into national affairs. But these are potential costs that could be overcome by successful efforts to build new trust and a new consensus between developed and developing states. And they are possible costs that have to be weighed against the effects of opposing the greater democratization of international relations. Weaker states in Third World regions are likely to resent attempts by their more powerful neighbors to dominate regional affairs, but the skills of "collective bargaining" that lesser states of the South have developed in their confrontation with the North can be brought to bear also in the negotiation of new regional orders.

For both the richer and the poorer states of the Middle East, the coming decade would appear to offer great opportunities to build enduring new relations within the region and with states outside the region. But how fully these opportunities are realized will depend on the capacity of fragile political structures to support the large economic tasks for which material resources now exist. The opportunities and the constraints are skillfully assessed by John Waterbury and Ragaei El Mallakh.

The Middle East and the New
World Economic Order

John Waterbury

Introduction

The premise of this essay is simple. Middle Eastern states will fail in the 1980s to develop a cohesive, cooperative, regional development strategy or a collective bargaining position in relation to the North. Consequently, they will fail to extract the best terms possible in interactions with the North. Some states with exceptional and perhaps temporary economic advantages will do better than others, but economic disparities in the Middle East and rivalries among emerging regional powers will limit both the intraregional and extraregional relations of its states to a network of bilateral deals.

The single most salient line of cleavage between Middle Eastern, especially Arab, states is that dividing the petroleum-rich from the petroleum-poor. It is this cleavage that will increasingly condition both relations among states in the region and the approach of each of those states to their pursuit of a better deal from the prosperous societies of the industrial North.

The major oil-exporting states, especially those with unparalleled foreign exchange reserves, are in many ways no longer Southern states at all. Their financial strength and international credit-worthiness are so remarkable that they have become a breed apart—the North of the South. Because they can sell as much of their principal export as they want and buy whatever they need with minimal regard to price, none of these oil-rich states feels obligated to adopt collective stances in bargaining with the North except on the question of the international pricing of crude petroleum. They can pursue their development needs regardless of the development activities of their neighbors—above all, those of their poor neighbors. Moreover, and with some exceptions, even when the oil-rich set their terms for petroleum pricing, they rarely do so in light of North-South considerations. Their goal has not been to promote a better deal for the South, but to get a better deal for themselves. By contrast, the obviously "Southern" states of the region, devoid of raw materials as strategically important as petroleum as well as of foreign exchange and international credit-worthiness, would like to see a greater sharing of the wealth within the region. Thus, a regional North-South dialogue is emerging, but one in which neither the rich nor the poor have adopted collective positions vis-à-vis one another.

At the same time, small but sensitized elites, especially among the poor states, have increasingly come to hope that the rich will use their temporary global weight, itself a function of world dependency on fossil fuels, to promote a major effort by the industrialized North to stimulate the economic development of the region as a whole through opening markets for regional exports, offering long-term capital investment and "soft" financing terms for supplies of capital goods and commodities, and transferring advanced technology and expertise. In other words, these currently isolated voices would like to see the oil-rich voluntarily join together to bargain for the region in North-South encounters and to recycle their surplus earnings through coherent, rational, regional growth efforts even if the oil-rich must cut back their own highly ambitious national development plans in the process.

Such regional altruism is not likely to emerge in the next decade, if ever. Too many factors—many of which will be explored in the following pages—militate against it. Regional disparities in economic development may well be more accentuated at the end of the 1980s than they are today, with the oil-rich investing lavishly in their own well-being while the poorer states flounder along in their wake as best they can. Over this period the privileged states will probably continue to deal with Northern partners on a state-to-state or a state-to-multinational-corporation basis, eschewing confrontation tactics that their poorer neighbors may come to advocate. In turn, the less privileged will seek their own deals individually with the regional rich and with Northern states or economic interests. This two-tiered alignment, with its emphasis upon the *separate* as opposed to the *collective* action of the region's states, will maximize the bargaining strength of the more coordinated Northern states of the Organization for Economic Cooperation and Development (OECD) and present the North with ample opportunities to play off various regional interests against each other. In sum, the North will probably have to concede far less to the Middle East within the context of the new world economic order than would be the case if the rich and poor states in the region were to present a solid front. Rather than hostile confrontation, trade wars, decoupling, or even attempts by individual states to pursue wholly autarkic development, the odds are that the North will face a divided and accommodationist Middle East throughout the 1980s.

While the basis for this argument will be set forth in detail in this study, it may be useful to summarize some of the main points at the outset. Fundamental among them is that Middle Eastern states or national policy-making elites are not, with rare exceptions, thinking in terms of the North-South confrontation at all. There is no blueprint or strategy for bargaining situations and no shared image of what would constitute a good or a bad deal. There is a certain irony to this state of affairs in that in good measure it was the collective action of the Arab oil-exporting states in 1973 that crystallized several of the most important economic issues in the North-South debate. But the fact is that the Arab oil embargo was instituted in the name of Arab solidarity against Israel and her foreign benefactors, not in the name of a better economic deal for the South. What we might call the prism of the Arab-Israeli conflict has consistently kept the Arab focus on geopolitical rather than economic issues. The lack of clarity in defining long-term economic issues serves to diffuse or post-pone the task of coming to grips with them.

In objective economic terms, Middle Eastern nations sort themselves out into at least four strata. If the criteria by which these strata are defined were consistently of operational signif-icance in policy formation and bargaining strategy, it would be within each stratum that one would expect to find the development of common policies in the pursuit or defense of common economic interests. In the first chapter of this study, we attempt to delineate these strata in order then to demonstrate the degree to which they fail to bear upon the elaboration of strategies. The poor and very poor among Middle Eastern societies have yet to attempt to close ranks for better terms either from the North or from the rich and very rich in the region itself. Likewise, the rich states with considerable potential for real economic growth have never acted as a bloc. It has been only those states with surplus foreign exchange that have acted, sporadically, in concert and have demonstrated a sense of shared interests and shared vulnerability.

Thus, two possible axes for collective action have been inconsequential since World War II and will probably remain so over the next decade. The first, pan-Arab unity, whether of a political or economic nature and regardless of the resource endowment of individual states, has receded as a practical reality almost in direct proportion to the vociferousness with which it has been acclaimed. No Arab state has yet sacrificed any significant national interest on the altar of Arab unity. All Arab regimes proclaim their devotion to the ideal, but each wants to impose its own terms, implicitly demanding that others accept the major sacrifices that unity would entail. Further, states with peculiar social characteristics (e.g., Lebanon, Jordan, and the Sudan, inter alia) fear absorption into larger units, while a handful of the super-rich would lose their regional financial leverage were economic integration to become a reality.

This kind of leverage has been incorporated in the various forms of clientage that the rich have been able to develop with the poor and very poor states in the region. One striking example that we shall examine below is that of Saudi Arabia's growing influence over Egypt and the Sudan. To perpetuate dependency linkages, the rich must deal as much as possible with individual states, following a tactic of divide and neutralize similar in many ways to Northern tactics toward the South. Indeed, the regional strength of these patrons is a function of the aggregate weight of their clients. In turn, each poor society is fueled by the hope that it may be the beneficiary of so much largesse that it need not concern itself overly with building effective horizontal, or "class," links with states of similar economic makeup. Collective action along this horizontal axis, unlike that of Arab unity, has seldom been proclaimed as desirable, nor has it been pursued any more frequently as a realistic goal. Instead, the present economic hierarchy of Middle Eastern societies has been maintained through the reinforcement of vertical dependency linkages between rich and poor that probably will be safeguarded in the years to come. The regional rich with large amounts of disposable foreign exchange are all, with the exception of Libya, sympathetic to "Western" goals and eager to avoid confrontation over global economic issues.

A number of factors enhance the ability of the super-rich to consolidate their position over the medium term. One has already been mentioned: the regional preoccupation with the Arab-Israeli dispute. Another is the ritual assertion that the Middle East is basically well-endowed and will ultimately be fully capable of providing for itself. There is consequently no sense of urgency, no feeling that time is running out nor that unique opportunities are being missed to develop the region as a whole or any of its states. Economic dependency, as far as the dependents are concerned, is a temporary phenomenon, one that will be overcome when real growth takes place. And almost without exception, growth is conceived of in national terms. Each state appears confident that it has the potential to build a viable national economy. To some extent there is also an unspoken and unspeakable assumption that one's neighbors, through incompetence, misguided policies, or congenital obtuseness, will fail in their own efforts, contributing thereby to the predominance of oneself. In short, most governments somehow expect to pull their chestnuts from the fire, regardless of what their neighbors do and, occasionally, directly at their expense. Thus there is a great deal of maneuvering for advantage at the subregional level, the ramifications of which will be described in Chapter Two.

Despite the lack of Middle Eastern focus on the issues of the global bargain, certain of the region's policy-making elites do participate in the various forums in which these issues are debated. The Organization of Petroleum Exporting Countries (OPEC) is foremost among them, but all will be given some attention in Chapter Three, for it is from them that a growing awareness of North-South questions is likely to spread. But such awareness will be long in coming, and in the meantime the amount of homework that goes into preparing for formal North-South encounters will remain inadequate. Correspondingly, the North will be able to deal with the Middle Eastern states piecemeal. Even nominally collective negotiations, such as the Euro-Arab dialogue, may, if they ever achieve practical results, distinguish Arabs of the Mediterranean littoral from the rest.

In most respects Middle Eastern states have not acted differently in the North-South context or in the regional context than have other developing states. Divided ranks and national policies of short-term expediency are the norm among the Southern states despite economic ills that would seem to dictate urgent collective action. Even OPEC, uniquely successful among Southern instruments for marketing raw materials, is built on a delicate balance of the foreign exchange needs and development strategies of its member nations. Declining prices, for instance, could pull it apart. In short, during the 1980s the Middle East will not contribute to the rise of a "Southern peril," but will instead bargain a little harder for the patronage that the North and its local protégés have always been willing to provide.

ONE

The Socioeconomic Stratification of Middle Eastern Economies

Middle Eastern states, while clearly not of the First World of capitalist, industrialized nations nor of the Second World of socialist, industrialized states, are not uniformly of the Third nor of the more recently conceived Fourth World (comprising states in which development has not even begun—Chad, for instance— or in which it appears structurally impossible to start—Bangladesh). No Middle Eastern economies are industrial in the sense of having the major contribution to their gross national product (GNP) come from manufacturing as opposed to extractive industries. Indeed, if revenues from the oil industry are excluded, the service sector, built around the sprawling public bureaucracies, tends to make the largest contributions to GNP. While industry employs a relatively low proportion of the work force, agriculture—except in Libya and the oil sheikdoms—constitutes the single largest sector of employment. At the same time, however, the ratio of output to labor in agriculture is far lower than in industry, where relatively few workers contribute a disproportionately large share of GNP. This situation merely reflects a tendency in the region to develop small capital-intensive industrial sectors while hardly improving extensive, backward, labor-intensive agricultural sectors. Bridging both are large public bureaucracies and public education systems reflecting a general conviction of the state's duty to provide welfare and regulatory services. Finally, interlacing the national economies are dense networks of predominantly private retail and wholesale traders. Again leaving aside oil, most countries of the Middle East have a similar composition of GNP and distribution of work forces. Moreover, the prominent if not dominant role of the state in economic and social life is accepted by nearly all regimes (Lebanon is or was the exception here) regardless of their political coloring.

One may add to the above general statements a few other socioeconomic "universals." Middle Eastern populations are growing at rapid rates: between 2.1 percent per year in Egypt (a rate that, if continued, would double population in 33 years) and 3.4 percent in Syria, Algeria, Iraq, and Morocco (a rate that, if continued, would double population in 20 years). Consequently, between 40 and 50 percent of the population in these countries is less than 16 years old, which places a heavy strain upon the productive sectors of society and at the same time presents an almost insurmountable obstacle to providing universal primary education. With the exception of the masses in Lebanon and Turkey, the majority of the region's inhabitants are illiterate and thus seriously impeded from participating in development efforts. Because of rapid population growth, the mountain of illiteracy in the Middle East has scarcely been eroded. Illiteracy and poverty are closely associated. High infant mortality rates, relatively low life expectancy, and poor nutritional levels characterize most of the area regardless of size of GNP and average per capita income. These latter two indices can be misleading because the distribution of national income is frequently highly skewed. That 5 percent of the population which earns the highest income in most Middle Eastern countries absorbs between 20 and 40 percent of national income. Even within relatively privileged groups, such as public employees in Egypt, the range between highest and lowest salaries is 26:1, or 40:1 if special allowances and bonuses are included.[1]

By all these measures, the societies of the Middle East conform

[1]See Dr. Galal Amin, "Income Distribution and Economic Development in the Arab World: 1959–1970," *L'Égypte contemporaine*, vol. 14, no. 352, April 1973, pp. 5–35, especially p. 18; idem, *The Modernization of Poverty: A Study in the Political Economy of Growth in Nine Arab Countries, 1945–1970*, E. J. Brill, Leiden, 1974.

to most of the criteria commonly adduced to define Third World states. Yet, according to these and other measures, there exist enormous disparities among these states. In Table 1, the nations of the area have been sorted into five groups. The first four have been determined according to purely economic considerations, while the group consisting of Jordan and Lebanon reflects the unique political and economic status of those states. The data entries for all countries have been selected to reflect the major differences and similarities among them. The most revealing differences are in per capita GNP and the ratio between exports and imports. In general, all entries should be taken as indicating general orders of magnitude rather than precise measurements. Wherever possible, post-1973 data have been used for those entries most sensitive to rising oil prices and world inflation. As a result, GNP, per capita GNP, and import-export bills are occasionally informed guesses. Conversely, in the same area, the table does not reflect the most recent changes in level of oil sales and world market prices for primary products and raw materials.

Algeria, Iran, Iraq, and Morocco comprise group I. All four states produce and export an important raw material: the first three, oil and natural gas; Morocco, phosphates. Their economies and particularly their export earnings are dominated by this fact. For example, 93 percent of Iran's export earnings, whose value is equivalent to about 80 percent of GNP, come from petroleum. In this respect, these states differ little from those of group II. They do differ, however, in the size of their populations and hence their domestic markets, their geographic size (their combined land area is nearly equivalent to that of the United States), agricultural base, industrial nucleus, relatively sophisticated transportation and communications infrastructure, relatively large numbers of skilled laborers, and competent technocratic and managerial elites. In short, any or all of these states have a fairly good chance of attaining some modicum of self-sustaining growth and prosperity after the oil or phosphates run out. Their leaders do not have to be reminded of this fact: All four states have already embarked upon concerted development plans to draw maximum benefit from what may be a temporary

TABLE 1

The Five Major Economic Groups (The Middle East Region)

Country/ Group	Population Million	Population Year	Life Expectancy 1965–1970	% Pop. Literate
Group I				
Algeria	15.7	1972	50.7	25–30
Iran	32.4	1974	50	35
Iraq	10.4	1973	51.6	20
Morocco	15.3	1973	50.5	15–20
Group II				
Kuwait	K } .475 F } .515	1975 1975	68.6	47
Libya	2.257	1973	52.1	27
Oman	.600	1971	n.a.	n.a.
Qatar	.127	1971	n.a.	n.a.
Saudi Arabia	7.487[a]	1971	42.3	10–15
United Arab Emirates	.235	1971	n.a.	n.a.
Group III				
Egypt	38.0	1975	52.7	35
Sudan	17.3	1975[b]	n.a.	10–15
Syria	7.12	1974	52.8	35–40
Tunisia	5.6	1974	51.7	35
Turkey	38.2	1974	53.7	50
Group IV				
Mauritania	1.29	1973	n.a.	5
North Yemen	5.9	1971	42.3	10
South Yemen	1.63	1973	42.3	10
Somalia	3.09	1973	n.a.	5
Group V				
Jordan	2.6	1974	52.3	40
Lebanon	2.8	1974[c]	64.1	86

PRINCIPAL SOURCES: *International Financial Statistics*, November 1975; United Nations, *Statistical Year Book*, 1974; Charles Issawi, "The Economy of the Middle East and North Africa: An Overview," prepared for Committee on Critical Choices for Americans, June 1975 (unpub.); *World Bank Annual Report: 1975*; Sayyid Mar'ei and Sa'ad Hagras, *If the Arabs Want It*, Dar al-Ta'awan, Cairo, 1975.

GNP ($ million/yr.)		Per Cap. GNP ($)	% Labor Force in Agric.	% Contribution Agric. to GDP 1971	Value of Exports/yr. ($ millions)	
7,400	1974	525	76	12	4,670	1974
30,400	1974	940	42	15	24,200	1974
4,150	1973	400	48	21	6,776	1974
6,000	1974	375	54	31	1,769	1974
5,300	1973	5,353	1	—	8,966	1974
5,640	1973	2,515	35	2[d]	6,846	1974
700	1974	1,000	n.a.	n.a.	n.a.	
1,500	1974	10,000	n.a.	n.a.	n.a.	
30,000	1974	3,700[a]	72	6	28,000	1974
3,000	1974	10,000	n.a.	n.a.	n.a.	
10,000	1974	275	57	25	1,482	1974
2,000	1974	120	78	35	350	1974
2,300	1973	320	62	22	762	1974
1,920	1974	340	41	17	794	1974
13,000	1974	350	72	28	2,363	1974
260	1973	200	90	n.a.	159	1973
600	1974	90	89	n.a.	8	1973
200	1973	125	78	n.a.	121	1973
210	1973	70	89	n.a.	48	1973
800	1973	307	35	17	140	1974
2,100	1973	750	55	8	351	1973

[a]Estimates of the Saudi population range between 4 and 12 millions.

[b]A 1973 census put the population at 14.9 millions, but this is considered a major underestimate.

[c]There has been no census in Lebanon since 1936. The 1974 figure is an estimate.

[d]In 1960.

31

TABLE 1 (continued)
The Five Major Economic Groups (The Middle East Region)

Country/ Group	% Made Up of Oil, Cotton, Etc.	Value of Imports ($ million/yr.)		Public Debt Servicing as % of Exports		
Group I				1967	1973	1976
Algeria	89 oil	4,127	1974	6.0	2.3	15.0
Iran	93 oil	5,120	1974	4.9	10.6	n.a.
Iraq	95 oil	756	1974	0.9	3.0	n.a.
Morocco	54 phos.	1,974	1974	7.3	9.7	8.5
Group II						
Kuwait	96 oil	1,274	1974	n.a.	n.a.	n.a.
Libya	98 oil	2.262	1974	n.a.	n.a.	n.a.
Oman		n.a.		n.a.	n.a.	n.a.
Qatar		n.a.		n.a.	n.a.	n.a.
Saudi Arabia	99 oil	1,136	1973	n.a.	n.a.	n.a.
United Arab Emirates		n.a.		n.a.	n.a.	n.a.
Group III						
Egypt	45 cotton	2,297	1974	19.7	34.6[e]	n.a.
Sudan	43 cotton	627	1974	5.6	11.1	n.a.
Syria		1,202	1974	11.6	7.3	n.a.
Tunisia		976	1974	20.8	13.8	10.0
Turkey		5,893	1974	16.4	10.4	n.a.
Group IV						
Mauritania	72 iron ore	153	1973	n.a.	n.a.	n.a.
North Yemen		125	1973	n.a.	n.a.	n.a.
South Yemen		170	1973	n.a.	n.a.	n.a.
Somalia	50 animals	97	1973	n.a.	n.a.	n.a.
Group V						
Jordan	38 phos.	436	1973	1.8	3.7	n.a.
Lebanon		849	1973	n.a.	n.a.	n.a.

[e]Figure does not include Egypt's servicing of military debts.

Gross Investment as % of GDP		Average Per Cap. Elec. Energy Consumption in 1972 (kwh)	Grams Protein per Person per Day (1968)
1966–1968	1970		
18	30	533	46
19	19ᶠ	954	60
16	17ᵍ	642	60
14	15	223	62
18	15ʰ	10,441	n.a.
20	25ⁱ	4,407	n.a.
n.a.	n.a.	n.a.	n.a.
n.a.	n.a.	n.a.	n.a.
16	21ⁱ	900	62
n.a.	n.a.	n.a.	n.a.
19	9	324	69
10	14ʰ	n.a.	63
17	14ᶠ	455	75
22	22	349	67
17	18ᶠ	n.a.	91
n.a.	n.a.	n.a.	n.a.
n.a.	n.a.	23	n.a.
n.a.	n.a.	423	n.a.
n.a.	n.a.	n.a.	56
16	20ⁱ	331	65ʲ
23	18ⁱ	889	n.a.

[f]Percent of GNP.

[g]Percent of 1969 GNP.

[h]1969.

[i]1968.

[j]Comparable rates are 106 grams per day in the United States, 100 in Italy, and 79 in Japan.

advantage. That Morocco and Algeria, and to some extent Iraq and Iran, are locked in struggle for subregional economic and political dominance, as discussed below, is a logical consequence of their ambitions.

In marked contrast with what might be called classic Third World states, those of group I are credit-worthy. Because of their valuable exports their currencies are convertible, they have access to the Eurodollar market and Western banking institutions, and they are able to service their large external debts and pay for the massive imports of capital goods, technology, and know-how that they need for their development plans. They also can and do buy substantial amounts of arms, which may fuel their impulse toward striving for hegemony. What they do not have are large amounts of surplus earnings from their exports. Development and military needs generally absorb most of what they earn abroad, although Iran has been able to provide other countries of the region with substantial sums in commercial credits and soft loans. And in 1975 all four felt the pinch of the relative decline in demand for oil and phosphates and the additional absolute drop in world market prices for oil.[2]

The inclusion of Morocco in this group warrants an added comment. A few years ago, when phosphates sold at approximately $15 a ton, the general configuration of the Moroccan economy would have required Morocco's inclusion in group III. In the middle 1960s, Morocco's per capita income was lower than Egypt's and the country was struggling to meet its foreign obligations. There seemed to be no likelihood that the country could become an economic rival of its immediate neighbor, Algeria. But Morocco exports about one-third of all the phosphates traded annually in international markets, making it the world's major exporter. From that strategic position, the Office Cherifien des Phosphates, the state-run Moroccan phosphate monopoly, was able to quadruple export prices in 1974 and force other exporters to fall in line. Morocco's hard currency earnings

[2]Iran's oil production fell by about 15 percent in 1975, causing a curtailment of aid outlays and a more modest increase in the 1976 development budget than the 26 percent that had been planned.

soared, reaching perhaps $1 billion over the first 12 months of the price hike. This dramatic reversal in Morocco's economic fortunes and international credit-worthiness explains its inclusion in group I. Phosphates, however, may prove a more fragile underpinning for further development than oil and gas. Already world prices for phosphates have dropped substantially, and Morocco has had to cut back production. Yet if the country is able to institutionalize its hold over the Spanish Sahara, which is rich in phosphates, its continued inclusion in group I will be assured.

In the eyes of many Middle Easterners, the members of group II are not really "economies" at all and perhaps not even viable states. They are the artifact of the oil boom, for without oil even Saudi Arabia, the largest of them, would have about as much economic viability and regional clout as Mauritania. So much more so for Libya, Kuwait, Qatar, the United Arab Emirates, and Oman. These countries all have small (not to say minuscule) populations, small internal markets, little agriculture, no industrial base, little infrastructure where needed, no skilled work force, and only a smattering of technocrats and managers. They do have the capital to attract the people they need from other countries. Saudi Arabia relies upon hundreds of thousands of Omanis and Yemenis as laborers, upon Egyptians as schoolteachers and doctors, and upon a polyglot mixture of Arabs and non-Arabs in various sectors of the state bureaucracy. In Kuwait, the majority of the population, which is growing by 3.8 percent a year because of immigration, is foreign. Palestinians and Egyptians occupy strategic positions throughout the bureaucracy, educational system, and university. Qatar and the sheikdoms of the United Arab Emirates are in a similar situation. While there is some dispute as to just how large the Saudi population really is (some consider the current figure of approximately 8 million to be highly inflated), the aggregate population of group II in 1975 was probably no more than 10 million. Yet the aggregate GNP of this group is only slightly less than that of group I, which has 74 million inhabitants. Even more striking is the comparison with group III, whose aggregate population of 105 million is 10 times that of group II and whose aggregate GNP is one-third

35

less. The members of group II have massive surplus earnings from oil exports. These are earnings that for a variety of reasons—inadequate infrastructure, lack of investment opportunities, etc.—could be expended in the domestic economy only through elaborate contrivances such as development schemes of astronomic cost or the ostentatious acquisition of arms. As Sheikh Ahmed Zaki Yamani, Saudi Arabia's Minister of Petroleum and Mineral Wealth, has remarked, it is easier to find oil in the Arabian peninsula than water. But even Saudi Arabia's gigantic five-year investment plan, if fulfilled, would fail to absorb all the country's surplus earnings. Over the short and medium term, the existence of these surpluses endows the states of group II with a regional, not to say global, influence that they would never have had otherwise. Over the long term, it is unlikely that any of them, with the possible exception of Saudi Arabia, will be able to build self-sustaining economies or polities once the oil and the surpluses run out.

With group III we enter the Third World as it is conventionally conceived. On the one hand, these states are reasonably well endowed with roads, railroads, ports, skilled labor and an educated cadre, and relatively extensive domestic markets. But on the other hand, they do not share the international credit-worthiness of groups I and II. This inability to obtain external financing is crucial: In most respects these states have the same potential for growth as the states in group I, but they lack the ability to finance that growth. All are exporting nations, but Egyptian and Sudanese cotton, Tunisian olive oil, or Turkish labor simply cannot earn as much foreign exchange as oil and gas. All of these countries have faced periods of chronic external indebtedness and have had to commit some of their meager foreign exchange earnings to debt servicing. Egypt is the "leader" in this respect, using approximately 40 percent of export earnings to service its public external debt. Needless to say, a country's indebtedness or credit-worthiness inevitably has major repercussions on the manner in which it conducts itself in relation to other nations.

The countries in group III are not unique in their varying

dependency upon imported food, but having to pay for those imports in hard currency further reduces the ability of these states to import capital goods and technological expertise. In this regard, too, Egypt is the most vulnerable: Its rate of population growth has begun to outstrip the ability of the agricultural sector to meet basic food needs. While all of the five societies in this group have ailing agricultural sectors, in Turkey, Syria, and the Sudan the possibilities for improvement are great. In Tunisia, and especially Egypt, which has already developed its agricultural base to a very high level, there is less that can be done. Each further increase in production is achieved only at high cost. Moreover, it is not certain that any amount of technological change in the countryside, whatever its cost, could meet the demands for employment and food of a large and growing population that even today lives in rural regions more densely populated than those in Java or Bangladesh. With both countries taxing the carrying capacity of their available land, the shift to an industrial economy is not simply a planner's option but a national necessity—unless Tunisia wishes to evoke its Phoenician origins and, like Lebanon, become a mercantile state. The economic malaise of this group is reflected in the per capita income of its members, which, ranging from $120 to $350 per year, falls below the lowest of the average of group I and is completely dwarfed by the super opulence of group II. Even then, statistics on average per capita income reveal nothing about actual distribution. The bulk of the Egyptian population, for instance, probably earns closer to $150 a year than $275.

Group IV is what group II would be if it did not have oil. That statement in itself is something of an injustice to the four states in this group, for any one of them would have far greater claims to economic viability than an oil-less Kuwait, Qatar, or Abu Dhabi. But since group IV countries do not have oil, they not only are the poorest societies of the region but also find themselves on the periphery of the Arab and Mediterranean worlds. Their combined GNP is one-fourth of Kuwait's, while their combined population is 10 times greater. Their per capita incomes range from $70 to $200 per year. Their populations are overwhelmingly rural and illiterate. Single commodities—iron ore for Mauritania or animals for Somalia—dominate the exports of some countries, while the economies of other states have no exports at all. South Yemen, for instance, is dependent upon the volume of traffic in the port of Aden. While under different circumstances and in a different ideological context Aden could become the Middle Eastern's version of Singapore, the stark reality of the contemporary situation is that South Yemen, North Yemen, Somalia, and Mauritania are the Fourth World of the Middle East: peripheral, impoverished, and grossly underfinanced.

Any categorization brutalizes reality, but even the preceding quadrifold distribution inadequately reflects the variety of Middle Eastern societies. There is no acceptable way to include Lebanon or Jordan in any of the preceding four categories largely because their economic characteristics are so closely linked to their unique political status. Jordan would have been an easy candidate for group III had not its economic heart, the West Bank, fallen under Israeli occupation in 1967. Jordan's economy is a truncated one, and although what remains of it is doing fairly well, Jordan must rely on outside aid for survival. Lebanon is a very different case. Until the recent months of communal fratricide, it had affirmed its role as a regional clearinghouse emporium, banking center, and political refuge. Its highly educated, generally prosperous population thrived on transaction trade, brokerage, and supply for all its neighbors. At this point, however, the possibility of Lebanon's ever again filling that role is moot; but if it is to do so, its unique status among all Arab states will have to be confirmed once again by the Arab League.

The economic makeup of these five groups has direct bearing upon the manner in which their constituent members perceive their regional and extraregional roles. At the same time, the characteristics shared by states within each group should not imply and in fact do not entail any effective coordination among them. The categorization is that of an outside observer, and any impression that what has been described are "blocs" should be dispelled. These categories are merely devices to illustrate the diversity in economic characteristics among Middle Eastern societies in order to emphasize that they are not all roughly alike. Nonetheless, the categorizations do suggest subgroups of states that might band together *if* they were aware that they shared similar assets and liabilities in their pursuit of national growth. Shared statistical characteristics alone, however, have not been sufficient to bring together the members of each category.

TWO

National Development and Regional Options

PROSPECTS FOR REGIONAL INTEGRATION

The Arab states of the Middle East have been for decades self-proclaimed advocates of achieving integral unity and overcoming "superficial" divisions.[3] If the ideal had been honored or realized, then the Middle East would now form a mostly solid front in North-South negotiations. However, finding the formula for the integration that all proclaim desirable has proven extremely difficult. Union has too often been conceived as a means for a state to improve its national prospects while making minimal sacrifices to the larger entity. Inasmuch as all parties have, with rare exceptions, sought such terms, regional integration has remained a distant goal. What, then, are the bases for greater Arab unity, and what are the national considerations that have overridden them? How do various regimes assess the need or desir-

[3]In the following discussion of national and regional developments treatment of Turkey will be cursory, since that country's self-selected field of action has been the Aegean and the economic realm of the European Economic Community. Turkey cannot ignore its southern Arab flank if only because it must take cognizance of the fact that it controls important sea and overland routes between the Soviet Union and the Arab world. Turkey also controls the headwaters of the Euphrates and must, therefore, deal with Iraq and Syria. It lies astride increasingly important overland transit routes for goods pouring into Iran and the Persian Gulf area. But Turkey's current vocation is not Middle Eastern or Arab but European and Balkan.

ability for integration? What states are so endowed that they can safely ignore questions of merging with larger entities? Could the Arab world, even if it were to integrate, provide for its own development?

The Arabs are the sixth power of the world.
President Anwar el-Sadat

Without oil, the Arab world is the poorest region of the globe.
Mohammed al-Imam, Council for Arab Economic Unity (CAEU)

These two observations are both reasonably accurate and do not contradict one another. The Arab world and Iran could make it alone because they control the greater part of the world's proven oil reserves. Going it alone means that the Arab states and Iran have the financial wherewithal to invest massively in the modernization of agriculture, in the exploitation of existing resources, and in the transfer of basic industries and technology. They have the aggregate population, strategic location bordering the sea, land and air routes to practically everywhere, and the arms to be a world power in the geopolitical sense. But today, the Arab world is no more a world power than Latin America and no more integrated than sub-Saharan Africa. The area's economic *potential* is still only that. The all too obvious fact is that only some Middle Eastern states have large oil and gas reserves. They fall into groups I and II of the schema presented in Chapter One, and their perceptions of the need for regional integration and the possibility of autonomous national growth differ considerably from those of the members of groups III and IV, but not of group V.

Unlike the Latin Americans and the black Africans, Arab elites have been obsessed and bedeviled by the quest for unity, integration, and the submersion of more parochial national loyalties into the *marmite* of the Arab nation. These themes have also penetrated deeply into the consciousness of the Arab masses. The promoters and advocates of Arab unity after World War II were the politicians and, eventually, heads of state who

42

sought political and military solidarity to thwart the divide-and-rule tactics of neoimperialist forces. Their preoccupation was with global bipolarity and the cold war, Soviet or United States spheres of *political* influence, military alliances, and of course, confrontation with Israel. Unity or integration for the promotion of regional development was an important but secondary concern throughout the 1950s and 1960s.

In this vein several attempts were made at political unity, all of them unsuccessful: Egypt-Syria, Egypt-Syria-Iraq, Jordan-Iraq, Sudan-Egypt, Syria-Egypt-Sudan-Libya, Egypt-Libya, Tunisia-Libya, and North and South Yemen. It has also been bruited about that Saudi Arabia and North Yemen may unite. As failures accumulated and continue to accumulate, important strategic divergences emerged that have direct bearing on current proposals for *economic* unity. It was undoubtedly President Gamal Abdel Nasser who, in the wake of the dissolution of the United Arab Republic in 1961, gave prominence to the notions that unity could not take place among dissimilar regimes, that sharing an "Arab heritage" was not in itself compelling enough to lead to unity, and that progressive, socialist states (namely, Egypt) could not conceivably unite with reactionary states such as Saudi Arabia under the thumb of neoimperialist forces and the international oil cartel (the Seven Sisters). Ideological and sociostructural homogeneity, in this view, must precede harmonization and coordination, not to speak of unity. Nasser had to stifle such views after 1967, when his foreign exchange budget became dependent on the annual subsidies of his erstwhile ideological adversaries: Saudi Arabia, Kuwait, and Libya.

Another point that has consistently been at issue among proponents of integration is the notion of an Arab world of states as against an Arab world of Arabs. At stake has been the quest for radical integration and the birth of a single Arab nation as against the more cautious goal of unity among the constituted states of the region. Almost from its inception more than three decades ago, the Baath party of Syria, standard-bearer of radical integration, considered the League of Arab States (Arab League) an impediment to real unity—not a catalyst—for it consecrated the artificial boundaries and subregional identities that colonial regimes had so carefully nurtured. If unity was the objective—and Baathis and non-Baathis alike agreed that it was—then, they argued, it could not be achieved within the context of regional nation-states taking timid and inconsequential steps in the right direction. It could not be expected that states of differing size and economic makeup, widely differing ideologies and political regimes, and links of varying intensity with one or another of the great powers would surrender national prerogatives in the name of the Arab collectivity. Consequently, it was argued that Arab national unity had to be achieved or imposed radically, and on the basis of an ideologically consistent revolutionary strategy. More moderate national elites argued for "incrementalism"—the adoption of small measures whose cumulative impact over time would be to reduce political and economic differences among states until they would be no greater than those among members of the European Economic Community (EEC).

For the majority of Arabs these are still the most salient options. Yet, in the face of so many failures, there is a widespread skepticism about the prospects for political unity of any kind. Until recently, new forces for unity and integration—the planners and economists—have been lost in the shuffle. What they hope to achieve may well depend upon the regime they serve,[4] but their emphasis is distinctly and emphatically upon economic problems and goals. These technocratic elites are the new blood of Arab unity, and to them has fallen the task of devising strategies for moving toward integration and dealing with the North. For the last 20 years, a growing number of them have learned that the terms of trade, the terms of borrowing, the role of multinationals, and the flow of investment are more important than the North Atlantic Treaty Organization (NATO), the Central Treaty Organization (CENTO), the Black Sea fleet, or possibly even Israel.[5]

---

[4]The managers and technocrats are nowhere in power in the Middle East, but the one such figure who has made policy and shaped national growth strategies is Abdessalm Belaid, former Minister of Industry and Petroleum in Algeria. Dr. Aziz Sidqi, long-time Minister of Industry in Egypt in the 1960s, represented a similar force.

[5]For one who suggests that this may be the case, see Muhammed Sid-Ahmad, *After the Guns Fall Silent*, St. Martin's Press, New York, 1976.

Like the politicians and ideologues, however, the planners and technocrats are divided over the question of appropriate strategies. The moderates again advocate a step-by-step approach toward economic integration, carefully safeguarding national economic sovereignties in the process. They envision the development of an Arab common market with customs unions and progressive reduction of inter-Arab tariffs, free movement of labor and capital, and other mechanisms modeled on those of the EEC. They suggest further that coordination of national development plans may promote more profound forms of integration. This school probably represents the mainstream in current thinking. Many persons who assume radical and conservative positions on other issues are united in affirming inviolable national sovereignties. In general, reducing formal sovereignty will prove extremely difficult, since most states in the area have only recently acquired their independence, and national identity within some states is still fragile.

By contrast, an increasingly important group of analysts have put forward arguments that run directly counter to the gradualist proposition. Their point is simple: The Arab world does not have the time to wait for gradualist solutions that would not produce integration anyway. The region has a unique opportunity to achieve prosperity, an opportunity that will be irretrievably lost if surplus oil earnings are not immediately put to work for all Arabs. Some derogation of national sovereignties is a vital necessity. Planners must think of people not as citizens of country X but as Arabs. Free trade areas and customs unions established within the nation-state framework will impede rather than promote regional integration because any and all concessions will be made purely to satisfy national self-interest. If the concessions are wisely made, they will reinforce national sovereignties. If there are any doubts whether concessions will enhance national interests—as in the case of protecting local industries by tariff barriers or allowing the free movement of capital and labor—they probably will not be made at all.

The brief history of the Arab Common Market would seem to confirm this school's hypothesis. The Market came into operation in 1965 as a nucleus of Arab states to which others have adhered over time. Efforts to reduce tariffs on manufactured goods proved futile because the Arab states had similar industries (e.g., textiles and processed foods). Between 1965 and 1970, trade among member states increased by only 1 percent and actually declined 12 percent among nonmembers. While major actors in the Market—Syria, Iraq, and Egypt—pursued policies of national self-sufficiency, others increased their trade outside the region. In the period 1966–1970, Arab trade with the United States increased by 111 percent, with the Federal Republic of Germany by 156 percent, and with the United Kingdom by 150 percent. As the source of these figures notes, these were the countries most hostile to the Arabs.[6]

The principal promoter of the Arab Common Market has been the Council on Arab Economic Unity, established in 1964, and now presided over by Dr. Abd al-'Al Sakban of Iraq. The CAEU is charged with promoting economic unity among member states through tariff reductions, development of free trade zones, encouragement of intra-Arab investment, promotion of free movement of labor, and the rational distribution of industries. A number of analysts at the Council, perhaps because of their intimate connection with the Common Market, wish to move on to much more ambitious projects emphasizing multinational approaches. At an initial stage these would be aimed at the *mis-en-valeur* of existing natural resources. This is a crucial preliminary state to more directly productive ventures. The vehicles proposed to mobilize the capital and know-how necessary to the success of big regional projects are public (in the sense that they would be

[6]Dr. Ahmad Faris Murad, "The Evolution of Economic Construction and the Growth of Commercial Exchange as Two Approaches to Arab Economic Integration," paper presented to the Seminar on Long-Term Planning and Regional Integration in the Arab World, Institute of National Planning, Cairo, January 14–21, 1976, p. 19, in Arabic. The author is from the Arab Planning Institute, Kuwait. Somewhat different figures are presented by Dr. Fa'iq 'Abd al-Rasul, "Economic Blocs—A Path to Rapid Growth and Economic Integration," *Petroleum and Development* (Baghdad), vol. 1, no. 2, 1975, pp. 79–101. He states that among the five founding members of the Common Market, the value of exports rose from $78 million to $175 million between 1964 and 1973, and imports from $87 million to $204 million. But this still represented only 2.6 percent of the total exports of those states and 4.2 percent of total imports (p. 100).

under the control of the Arab states) multinational corporations. In the view of Mohammed al-Imam, this approach to a new regional order will have effects more far-reaching than changes in the terms of trade and financing with the outside world. In addition, the sponsorship of regional projects under regional guidance would impel the Arabs beyond problems of technology transfer into a stage where they would need to create their own technologies.

Since 1973 the CAEU has seen its ranks swelled by nearly all the members of the Arab League. Moreover, a number of multinational schemes are now in existence or being planned: the Arab Fund for Economic and Social Development (AFESD), the Arab Company for Petroleum Investments, the Arab Navigation Company, the Arab Maritime Services Company, the Arab Payments Fund, and companies for livestock, mining, and pharmaceuticals. Under study are projects for petrochemicals, fertilizers, and cement. There now also exist an Arab Corporation to Guarantee Investments and another to guarantee credits. Finally, after the Rabat summit conference of 1974, it was decided to establish an Arab War Industries Organization, with its base in Egypt, to develop a regional munitions and armaments industry. The organization will be initially capitalized at about $1 billion, mainly from Saudi Arabia, Kuwait, and Qatar.[7]

The Council would like to see the Kuwait-based Arab Fund for Economic and Social Development, established in 1972, become its major financial and technical arm. A major test case for the philosophy of both the Council and the Fund is shaping up in the Sudan. The Sudan is one of the world's most important underexploited agricultural regions. It could add as many as 30 million acres of rain-fed and river-irrigated land under cultivation to the 10 million acres currently farmed.[8] The Arab world as a whole is a food-deficit area. Chronic shortages exist in food

[7]See the articles and reports on the Council's activities in the *Journal of Arab Economic Unity* (Cairo), vol. 1, no. 1, April 1975; and an interview with Dr. Sakban, "The Arabs and the Reality of Their Economic Unity," *Al-Ahram al-Iqtisadi*, July 15, 1975 (all citations from this periodical are in Arabic).

[8]Sayyid Mar'ei and Sa'ad Hagras, *If the Arabs Want It*, Dar al-Ta'awan, Cairo, 1975, pp. 137–155, in Arabic.

grains, edible oils, sugar, and livestock. The Arab Organization for Agricultural Development has conducted a regionwide survey emphasizing the potential for greatly increased grain (wheat) and animal production in Syria, Iraq, Morocco, and Somalia. The Sudan, with its warm climate and abundant rainfall (in the south), has been singled out for the production of sugar and edible oils (corn, sesame, and ground nuts) and the raising of livestock in the savannah areas. If the agricultural production of all these regions were incorporated in a regional plan, the Arab world could feed itself by the year 2000. The question is, once again, how rapidly surplus oil earnings can be mobilized toward this end.[9]

The Arab Fund has drawn up a comprehensive plan for Sudanese agriculture during the rest of this century. If the plan is implemented, the Sudan will be able to triple its agricultural exports and eventually provide 40 percent of the edible oil now imported by the Arab world, 20 percent of its sugar imports, and 50 percent of its meat imports. The plan will rely upon a combination of commercial and soft loans, long-term credits, and grants. The Sudanese, for their part, would have to raise about 40 percent of the investment load. The instrument proposed for the implementation of the plan is a multinational "authority" with virtually extraterritorial status in the Sudan (although the Sudan would be offered 10 percent equity in it); it would not be subject to nationalization and would own a major interest in all the projects under its auspices. Thus the Sudanese are being asked for a clear derogation of a portion of their economic sovereignty. If the Sudan goes along with the Arab Fund's formula, and it has officially decided that it will, the radical integrationists will have set an important precedent.[10] Or, as Mohammed al-

[9]Ibid; and Mahmud Riad, Secretary-General of the Arab League, "Before the Opportunity Is Lost," *Al-Ahram*, December 12, 1975; Dr. Mustapha Gabali, "The Necessity of Specialization and Integration in Agricultural Production among Arab States," *Al-Ahram*, January 17, 1974, and "The Food Problem in the Arab World," *Al-Ahram*, October 22, 1975. All citations from *Al-Ahram* are in Arabic. See also Dr. Kemal Ramzi Stino, Director of the Arab Organization for Agricultural Development, "The World Food Crisis and Its Impact Upon the Arab States," *Al-Kātib*, part 1, vol. 14, no. 163, October 1974, pp. 83–88, and part 2, no. 164, November 1974, pp. 53–58, in Arabic.

[10]It is important to remember that the non-Arab populations of the southern

Imam has argued, a step will have been taken to "outpace the national rush—especially in the oil-rich countries—toward purely national projects."[11]

The above notwithstanding, the momentum in the Arab world is in other directions, where narrow national self-interest still prevails. This is so because the majority of the states in the region, including Turkey and Iran, have sufficient human and natural resources to think that they can have regional integration with most of its advantages and few of its sacrifices, while another set—all the members of group II except Libya—have grave misgivings about subsuming themselves in any larger unit. Finally, even those states such as Egypt whose very survival would seem to depend on integration still cherish the symbol and hope of self-sufficiency. At a distance, one can easily argue that self-sufficiency and economic sovereignty are myths; that if all the states are bent on establishing basic industries, modernizing agriculture, exporting and earning foreign exchange, moving into advanced technology, and so on, they will need to find markets, skilled labor, and managerial talents in the area. Not all Middle Eastern states can profitably maintain iron and steel complexes, but Algeria, Egypt, Tunisia, Iraq, Iran, and Turkey all try; Morocco plans to produce steel; and Saudi Arabia has grandiose aims in this (and practically all other) industrial areas. The same could be said for aluminum smelters, vehicle assemblies, textiles and—one day perhaps—petrochemicals and fertilizers. Little thought is being given to the areas of complementarity and the markets within the region. Just as Somalia's heavy investment in rice cultivation or Egypt's in sheep raising would be absurd (although conceivable), it makes little sense for each Middle Eastern state to replicate the industrial structures of the others.

Although the preceding remarks apply across the board, subsets of states have diverse economic options and imperatives.

Sudan, only recently emerged from years of fighting with the north, might be particularly apprehensive about the place of this "Arab" authority in shaping the Sudan's basic economic options.

[11]Mohammed al-Imam (CEAU), "Cooperation Among Developing Countries," in Alphonse Aziz and Mabid al-Jarhi, *The New International Economic Order and UNCTAD IV*, Institute of National Planning, Egypt, December 1975, memo 1129, p. 163.

Algeria, Iran, Iraq, and more recently Morocco have enough room for economic maneuvers so that any steps they take toward integration will be on terms most advantageous to themselves. While all these nations but Iran, for whom the problem is irrelevant, pay at least lip service to Arab unity, they have all (with the exception of Morocco, which is too new at this game to have affirmed its status yet) devised development plans in light of their will to be one of (or predominant among) the major economic and military powers in their subregion: i.e., the Maghreb; the Fertile Crescent; and the Arabian peninsula, including the Arab shores of the Persian Gulf (henceforth simply referred to as the Gulf). We shall return to this point below.

The states of group II are incontestably wealthy enough, temporarily, not to have to worry about integration. In fact, their power in the region, however fragile, would be lost through integration because they would be compelled, rather than merely asked, to bankroll other states' development. Libya, which has frenetically sought to lose itself in the embrace of some other Arab nation since 1969, is a striking exception to this generalization. One wonders how much this impulse is dependent upon the personal will of Colonel Muammar al-Qaddafi. For the others—Kuwait, Saudi Arabia, the Emirates, Qatar—the situation is fraught with equally unpalatable alternatives. Saudi Arabia is undeniably powerful not because of its economic potential but because it can finance powerful clients such as Egypt. Without this, or some other equally imposing client, Saudi Arabia would have little regional leverage. Not surprisingly, it has no wish to sign away this leverage in the name of the Arab nation, regional development, and more equitable regional income distribution. These states derive their power from the gap between rich and poor nations and the recurrent need of the latter to drink from the trough of the rich—access to which is a privilege, not a guaranteed right. Their relations with their poor neighbors are analogous to those between North and South generally, except that the Arab North has no power other than its purse strings.

Yet the most dependent among the Arab nations are unwilling to face this fact. Many Egyptian policy makers, for instance, believe that they can produce an economic take-off by effecting only a few changes: an end to the war and the "hemorrhage"

50

of defense spending; a few technological innovations by which
the desert can be conquered; a few temporary capital transfusions
from the Arab rich; the discovery of a little oil; increases in
tourism and Canal traffic; and greater access to foreign markets,
somewhere, for the country's manufactured goods. Yet Egypt's
38 million persons, who are expected to grow to 65 to 70 million
by the year 2000, are today living on only 6 million acres of
already overburdened land. Egypt imports more than $2\frac{1}{2}$ million
tons of grain and flour annually, a figure that can only rise in the
future.[12] While foreign indebtedness, now consuming approximately 40 percent of export earnings in annual servicing obli-
gations, can be reduced, that reduction will be only a slight one
if the import bill continues to outstrip the economy's ability to
export. In short, one would expect to see Egypt throwing all its
massive, if disheveled, bulk into the quest for regional integration. But Egypt-firstism is a more prominent theme in Egypt
today than Arabism. The prospects in Tunisia, Syria, the Sudan,
and Turkey are better than those in Egypt, but these nations,
too, need to sell abroad in order to pay for their development
needs and food imports. Turkey and Tunisia, like Egypt, must
export labor to generate foreign exchange and alleviate unemployment, while the Sudan, like Saudi Arabia and Kuwait, must
import labor.

The economically destitute nations of group IV do not constitute a force for Arab unity, although, curiously, two of them—
Somalia and South Yemen—are governed by the only Marxist
regimes in the Arab world. However warmly these states may
feel toward the goal of integration, they are all geographically
and economically marginal to the Arab world. Egypt is a big,
poor nation with a proportionately large army; its poverty is a
source of bargaining power. The capacity to twist arms, however,
is largely denied the members of group IV, which have little
more than their poverty and strategic location.

Algeria embodies all the contradictions of the present situation.
It has championed the right of states to dispose of their natural
resources as they see fit, a principle for which it locked horns

[12]See John Waterbury, "'Aish: Egypt's Growing Food Crisis," *AUFS Report*, Northeast Africa Series, vol. 19, no. 3, March 1974.

with France from 1962 until 1971 over oil. Simultaneously, Algeria has urged that the members of OPEC establish a fund from their oil earnings to extend aid to Third World nations most affected by rising petroleum prices. Algeria suggests that contributions to this fund be made obligatory. But if the principle of complete sovereignty over natural resources continues to be espoused, how can the obligation be more than a moral one?

Among the oil-less Arabs, the answer to that question is simple: The oil is *Arab* oil, a gift of divine or other providence, which must be used for the benefit of all Arabs. Oil is a common resource and must be treated as such. But their argument is no stronger than their will to abandon their own national frames of reference on all other issues. The fundamental ambivalence in this position of the oil-less Arabs extends to their definition of the new world economic order. Egyptians have resolved the delicate issue of being Arab when the situation requires it by calling for an "Arab Marshall Plan" that would compensate Egypt for its extensive national and financial losses resulting from four military encounters with Israel. Egypt and Syria, they argue, have been economically devastated by their sacrifices for the Palestinians and Arabdom in general, and must be given the means to rebuild their economies. While Sayyid Mar'ei, President of Egypt's parliament and generally considered to be on the Egyptian right, is the most articulate proponent of this idea, it has rallied all shades of political opinion in Egypt. On the left, Lutfi al-Kholi has written of petrodollars and petroblood, pointing out that the Arab oil producers owe their fabulous earnings after 1973 to the blood shed by Egyptian and Syrian troops. The balance sheets in oil and blood, he suggests, require sweeping adjustment.[13]

In sum, most states of the Middle East, whatever they say about unity, nurture the hope of a special deal or the unstated satisfaction of economic advantage. This tendency applies to the search for special arrangements beyond as well as within the

[13]Mar'ei's proposal is fully presented in Mar'ei and Hagras, *If the Arabs Want It*, pp. 429–451; see also Lutfi al-Kholi, "Petro-dollars and Petro-blood," *Al-Ahram*, January 30, 1975.

region. The need for a new order is taken for granted in a world where the gap between rich and poor nations is widening, yet national policy is frequently geared to the assumption that the Arab credits and soft loans, the foreign investments, the break-through in exports or crop production that will put matters right are all within reach. Moreover, there is a general perception that the Arab world is rich, reflecting both Europe's traditional cov-etousness toward the region and the fabulous oil earnings of the 1970s. This perception gives rise to a feeling that basic decisions on integration are not really pressing and perhaps may never need to be made at all. Middle Eastern states will take effective steps toward regional integration only if driven to it out of eco-nomic or political necessity (namely, Egypt and Libya) or be-cause they believe they can achieve it on their own terms (Al-geria, Iraq, Saudi Arabia). The super-rich neither need nor promote integration, yet they would be indispensable to any plan for unity. The poor both need and occasionally promote inte-gration, but lack the leverage to bargain for it on their own terms.

MANEUVERING FOR ADVANTAGE AT THE SUBREGIONAL LEVEL

The search for the special deal reinforces the dependency of the poor states of the area on the rich and the dependency of all states in the region on outside powers. Those states that find themselves in a roughly clientelistic relationship with some re-gional or outside power may well believe that the situation is both temporary and aberrant. Solidarity among the states of the region is the accepted goal of the future, but some states jockey individualistically to get the best strategic position for the coming of the great day, while others seek to postpone that day as long as possible. Less enigmatically, it is in the interests of Saudi Arabia, Kuwait, Qatar, the United Arab Emirates, Jordan, and Lebanon to impede progress toward "radical" integration. Also, the United States, out of solicitude for Israel, concern over oil supplies, and determination to block Soviet penetration, is widely believed to favor a Middle East in which there is maximum tension among states. Thus, there is a political and economic logic to the position of the above-named states as clients of the United States and to their attempts, whenever possible, to patronize their own local clients in turn. This logic in no small measure explains Egypt's rapprochement first with Saudi Arabia and then with the United States and its dilemma of pursuing its old dream of Arab unity—a vital necessity over the long term—or serving the strategic ends of its patron(s)—which is vital in the short term. Conversely, countries such as Iraq, Algeria, and Iran, which are not in immediate need of patrons (although they are on the lookout for clients), hope in the long term to assure their own subregional supremacy.

Beggar-my-neighbor policies flow directly from the economic stratification of Middle Eastern regimes. The financially strong nations, having bought political strength through clients, will continue to use their financial weight to perpetuate clientage. Countries whose economic future is bright will not be motivated by short-term altruism to jeopardize it. The clients, for their part, believe that after exacting from their temporary patrons the benefits of dependency, they will eventually be able to break the bonds of clientage. Given the mixed motives of the states of the Middle East, it is not difficult to account for the absence of solidarities within economic strata—and, as will be argued below, for the absence of common, preformulated bargaining positions in North-South relations.

It is frequently argued by both radical integrationists and moderates that general political integration will be possible only after the achievement of integration within subregions that make economic sense. While definitions of economically sensible clusters may differ from one analyst to another, the following groupings are generally accepted as most feasible. The Fertile Crescent would include primarily Syria and Iraq. It would consist of the Tigris-Euphrates basin, ports on the Mediterranean and Gulf, a vast and poorly exploited agricultural base, abundant oil resources, and adequate labor and managerial resources. On its periphery are Lebanon, Jordan, and Kuwait. Lebanon all too clearly could be divided up and apportioned to interested parties; Jordan, whose justification as an independent state is intellectually challenging, could be absorbed by Syria or a new Palestine (or, as is the case with Lebanon, by Israel); and Kuwait could be absorbed by Iraq or Saudi Arabia. Some non-Kuwaitis believe that once the oil begins to run out, most Kuwaitis will leave the country and live off the investments they are making abroad.

Egypt, the Sudan, and Libya make up another logical subregion combining Libya's oil, Egypt's industry and human resources, and the Sudan's promising agricultural hinterland. It, too, would sit astride trade routes from the Mediterranean to the Indian Ocean and East Africa. North Africans, who like to think of Libya as part of the Maghreb, might object to this troika. Some observers believe that Maghrebi unity has been impeded by the clear economic superiority of Algeria. They argue that economic integration among North African states would promote unity, and suggest that the formation of a Tunisian-Lybian economic unit and a Moroccan–Spanish Saharan unit would, along with Algeria, create three roughly coequal economic actors within the region. Without Libya, however, Tunisia would be dwarfed.[14]

A last, loosely defined subregion would consist of the Arabian peninsula, including the Arab shores of the Gulf. Yet given the immensity of the area and, with the exception of North Yemen, its reliance on a single, nonagricultural resource, it is very difficult to see how this subregion could be realized in any practical sense. Clearly, whatever happens in this or the Fertile Crescent region will be influenced if not determined by the actions of one of the Middle Eastern "great powers": Iran.

With these subregional groupings in mind, we may now examine more closely the actions and aspirations of the various nations of the Middle East. In almost all instances we shall find that what economic logic would put together, politics and long historical memories keep apart.

The Maghreb

Until the mid-1970s, the fact that politics and long historical memories would impede economic cooperation among the states of Morocco, Algeria, and Tunisia (i.e., ex-French, and still at the elite level, Francophone North Africa) was buried. The out-

[14]See, inter alia, Fathallah Oualalou, "Le Maghreb nécessaire," *Lamalif*, no. 71, June–July 1975, pp. 9–18.

break of open conflict in the Spanish Sahara brought to the surface the long-submerged impediments to unity. The two moderate states of North Africa, Morocco and Tunisia, had pursued national independence and their relations with France and other powers through markedly accommodationist policies. Both states won their independence using relatively little violence; after independence, French economic and cultural interests were allowed to remain intact, though more so in Morocco than in Tunisia. By the late 1960s, Tunisia and Morocco had entered into association accords with the European Common Market; since then, both have actively sought direct European and other foreign investment in their economies.

Their mutual differences with Algeria stem directly from this pattern of development. Unlike the two French protectorates, Algeria was juridically an integral part of France. Inasmuch as the French were unyielding on the question of Algerian independence, the process of national liberation there was, of necessity, violent. But it need not, in the eyes of the Algerians, have been so protracted had Morocco and Tunisia not accepted independence in 1956, thereby emasculating a Maghrebi resistance front. Despite the granting of asylum for Algerian guerrillas in independent Morocco and Tunisia, the Algerians felt betrayed. Once Algeria became independent in 1962, it assumed the role of catalyst to a Maghrebi union that would, at least in matters of foreign policy, take a resolutely nonaccommodationist stance toward France and all other neoimperialist powers. But neither Morocco nor Tunisia, as the Algerians suspected, had much inclination to align their policies with Algeria's, so no steps toward integration were taken. Algeria was seen by the two moderate nations as a radical threat rather than a catalyst to unity. In fact, Algeria and Morocco entered into armed conflict over their undefined southwestern border in September 1963. The Moroccan army performed better than the Algerian army, and Algerian President Ahmed Ben Bella and his Defense Minister, Houari Boumedienne, turned to the Soviet Union for arms. As a result, Algeria's regional image became even more threatening.

When Boumedienne toppled Ben Bella in June 1965, he seemingly buried his major differences with Morocco. At a 1972 meeting of the heads of state of the Organization of African Unity (OAU), Rabat and Algiers formally settled their border dispute and drew up plans for the joint exploitation of the Gara Djebilet iron mines in Algeria, perhaps by moving the ore out through the Atlantic port of Agadir in Morocco. In turn, Morocco ceded the area of Tindouf to Algeria, a concession that won King Hassan II little popularity at home.

With hindsight, we can see that Boumedienne had anticipated the coming of a new age. He found inappropriate and inadequate the predominantly political definition Ben Bella had given Algeria's national identity and its role in the region and in the Third World as a whole. Boumedienne instead emphasized the economic development of Algeria, without which Algeria would have no credible international voice. The two themes of Algerian development after 1965 were (1) sovereignty over natural resources, which meant gradual state take-over of all phases of extraction, refining, and exportation of gas and oil (accomplished by 1971); and (2) rapid, heavy industrialization based on petrochemicals and steel. As long as Morocco was not pursuing a similar strategy and was instead relying on selective agricultural modernization schemes, agro-industries, and foreign investments in light industries, there was no need for Algeria to lose time in sterile political confrontations.

Many Moroccan leftists became convinced in the late 1960s that instead of opposing Morocco's "reactionary" monarchy, Algeria wished to perpetuate it. For King Hassan was so immersed in internal political balancing games that no coherent development strategy was likely to emerge. At the same time that Algeria was reinvesting 25 to 30 percent of its GNP, Morocco dawdled along at 11 or 12 percent. The long-term portent of this is that by the time Morocco wakes up to its own potential— for the Moroccan opposition, an awakening dependent on a change of regimes—Algeria will have established itself as the uncontested economic power of the southern Mediterranean.

The Algerians may well see national strength as more important than regional development, although they find it perverse that others should chide them for not interfering in a neighbor's internal affairs. Perhaps more important, and this point applies as well to the other subregional conflicts we shall examine, the Algerian regime has a sense of mission. It believes that in building its own strength, it will eventually be able to bring its neighbors into alignment with the policies it thinks are right and necessary.

Throughout the period of political détente with Morocco, Algeria was uncooperative on one issue: association with the Common Market. Here Algeria could have it both ways. On the one hand, because Algeria was part of France when the Treaty of Rome establishing the EEC was signed in 1957—Article 227 of the Treaty of Rome defined Algeria's unusual status—many of France's benefits within the Market carried over to independent Algeria. There was, in any case, no problem of entry into the Market for Algeria's major export, oil, and there were very few problems regarding wine. Furthermore, several hundred thousand Algerian migrant workers were employed in France and other Common Market countries. For all these reasons Algeria was, in a sense, more integrated into and dependent upon the EEC than its two neighbors, and in no particular rush to work out its own articles of association. Instead, Algeria demanded of its neighbors a common and tough bargaining position on all commodities and manufactured goods, the status of North African workers in Europe, and the regulation of capital flows. As had happened a decade earlier, Tunisia and Morocco bolted and accepted terms of association, based purely on trade, which Algeria would not condone. In so doing they played, whether consciously or not, directly into the European strategy of "the wings blocking the supremacy of the center."[15]

Algeria's costless intransigence had paid off, however, for once the EEC association accords with its two neighbors expired in 1974, two years of negotiations produced three separate but nearly identical agreements with the European Community in April 1976 covering trade, financial assistance, and migrant workers. One suspects, nevertheless, that the EEC has not entirely laid aside the strategy of the two moderate wings against the

[15] Robert Albioni, "The Integration of the Maghreb: Problems and Prospects," *The Atlantic Papers*, vol. 1, 1972, p. 21; see, in the same volume, Chadli Tnani, "The Maghreb Face to Face with the European Community," pp. 24–34.

"radical" center, which may reemerge in future rounds of negotiation. In the meantime, steps toward free trade areas and tariff reductions on manufactures traded among North African states have not progressed. Algeria argues that opening up her markets to Tunisian and Moroccan manufactures would be equivalent to putting her "national" industries in direct competition with the industrial giants of the EEC, as they act through their Moroccan and Tunisian affiliates.[16]

The Saharan Struggle

The unity of people, yes; the unity of the peoples of the Maghreb, yes, starting tomorrow; an Arab Maghreb for the benefit of the peasants, workers, an avant-garde youth who work for the people's prosperity, yes, tomorrow; we are ready to put everything in common for a Maghreb where the exploitation of the many by man will be banished, yes; an Arab Maghreb to end the servitude of the peasant, yes; an Arab Maghreb in which the worker will be free and responsible, not a simple oppressed wage earner, yes; an Arab Maghreb where the national economy will not be dominated by foreign capital, yes.

President Houari Boumedienne

At the beginning there was a simple commercial policy that was seemingly most beneficent to Algeria . . . but which ties the country to the capitalist camp. This choice did not call into question its Arab and Maghrebi orientations. Onto this policy was grafted an economic strategy that could only rely upon the capitalist market, and when this strategy was subsequently consolidated by the first four-year plan (1969–73), the result was not long in coming: rupture of the Maghrebi, then Arab fronts and a flight forwards to the larger circle of neutral and Third World nations, which, being without structure or responsibilities, affords room for all sorts of maneuvers. The presence of Algeria in Maghrebi and Arab forums no longer serves any purpose but to block decisions so that the contradiction between real motives and state propaganda will not be revealed.[17]

Abdullah Laroui, Moroccan historian

[16] In 1964 at Tangiers, a Permanent Committee for Cooperation among Maghreb States was established. Libya disassociated itself after 1969. The Committee has been unsuccessful in promoting major tariff reductions.

[17] Houari Boumedienne, quoted in *al-Moujahid*, June 20, 1975; and Abdullah Laroui, "Réflexions sur la politique extérieure de l'Algérie," *Lamalif*, no. 70, April–May 1975, p. 6.

Morocco and Algeria have reopened all their old political wounds in their struggle over the Spanish Sahara. Their respective motivations are too complex to allow easy generalizations, but each nation is aiming to achieve hegemony in North Africa. Laroui is not exaggerating when he claims that Algeria's development plans have intensified its links with the capitalist world. Like Iran and Iraq, Algeria has become a tremendous market for Western equipment, technology, expertise, turnkey operations, and so forth. The United States, through firms such as El Paso Natural Gas and Bechtel Corporation, has played a growing role in this market.[18] If Algeria's development effort succeeds, these linkages with the West will probably be strengthened rather than weakened. Algeria will need markets for its manufactures; southern Europe, as much as if not more than Africa and the Middle East, will be its target. Natural gas and to a lesser extent petroleum will be the backbone of Algeria's petrochemical industry and its primary export. Large supply contracts have already been negotiated with France and other European markets and plans for trans-Mediterranean pipelines for gas are being studied. One pipeline would ideally run through Morocco, across the Straits of Gibraltar, then on to Spain and France.[19]

These factors explain, at least in part, Algeria's hard terms

[18]See William Quandt, "Can We Do Business with Radical Nationalists? Algeria: Yes," *Foreign Policy*, no. 7, Summer 1972, pp. 108–131; and John Waterbury. "Land, Man, and Development in Algeria: Part III, The Four Year Plan," *AUFS Report*, North Africa Series, vol. 17, no. 3, March 1973. The Ministry of Industry and Petroleum has retained Arthur D. Little as its principal foreign consultant since 1964. On Algeria's development strategy and self-appointed role in Southern leadership, see Bruno Étienne, *L'Algérie, cultures et révolution*, Éditions du seuil, Paris, 1977, especially chapters 7 and 8.

[19]Algeria is the world's major exporter of natural gas. Its estimated reserves are 3,000 billion cubic meters, mainly at Hassi R'mel. Existing export contracts cover 20 billion cubic meters a year, with the United Kingdom, Gaz de France, and El Paso leading the way. Spain and Italy will also buy Algerian gas, but the important contract is a package deal for 15.5 billion cubic meters to a consortium of European gas companies, which has yet to be finalized. See Paul Balta, "Le Congrès d'Alger sur le gaz naturel," *Le monde*, June 29, 1974; and Rupert Cornwell, "Banking on a Natural Gas Future," *Financial Times*, May 7, 1975.

in negotiating its association with the EEC, for the relationship is likely to be a lengthy one. The bait Algeria is offering to Western Europe, especially France and West Germany, is not merely energy but a bargaining hedge to get out from under the thumb of United States energy "management" for the Atlantic community. Algeria will trade this room for maneuver in return for access of its manufactures to EEC markets, transfers of capital and technology on acceptable terms, and improvement of conditions of Algerian workers in Europe. The bargain is not unintelligent and the Algerians feel they have the basic strength to follow through with it. But through the seizure of the Spanish Sahara, Morocco may have upset the entire strategy.

In the wake of the energy crisis, Morocco found itself the world's major exporter of what was too hastily called "white gold": phosphates. Morocco's annual production of 18 million tons, of which 16 million tons are exported, leaves its major rivals—the United States with 8.6 million tons and the Soviet Union with 5 million tons—far behind. When fertilizer prices rose rapidly in 1973–1974, Morocco was able to set a new international price for phosphates of about $68 a ton, thus raising its export earnings from approximately $150 million to more than $1 billion. Morocco's ability to continue to corner the export market would be enhanced, to say the least, if it could control the Buqra' deposits in the Spanish Sahara. Those deposits could yield 10 billion tons of high-quality rock and 6 million tons of exports per year. Whether kept in the ground or exported, the phosphates in this deposit would give Morocco tremendous leverage in world markets.[20] Finally, the war in Angola, the radical change in Portugal, and the declining health of General Franco must have convinced Hassan II that Spain did not have the heart to risk a drawn-out encounter over the Sahara—especially if Morocco could offer compensation for Spain's withdrawal in the form of continued access to the phosphates, fishing rights, protection for Spanish enclaves on Moroccan soil (Ceuta and Me-

[20]Ann Crittenden, "Phosphates: Taking a Leaf from Oil's Book," *New York Times*, November 9, 1975; and "Une forte odeur de phosphate," *Révolution africaine*, no. 610, October 31, 1975.

lilla), and a moderate power in control of an area adjacent to the Canary Islands.

Whereas Morocco's goal is clearly to become Algeria's economic coequal, Algeria is bent on denying Morocco precisely that status. One must give some credence to Algeria's motives, which go far beyond respect for United Nations resolutions and concern for the peoples of the Sahara. Rather, Morocco's acquisition of the Sahara not only would further open northern Africa to European and American penetration (Spanish, American, French, and German interests are already there) but also would lead to the possible triumph of accommodationist policies toward the EEC.

Libya and Tunisia

Omitted from this discussion so far, and for cause, have been Libya and Tunisia. The commitment to moderation shared by Morocco and Tunisia has not been enough to make these two countries effective allies. Tunisia's President, Habib Bourguiba, came to power by abolishing a monarchical regime of sorts in 1957. This act hardly endeared him to King Hassan's father, Mohammed V of Morocco. Tunisia also recognized Mauritanian independence at a time when Morocco still laid claim to that territory as its own. Even though Morocco eventually did recognize the new state, old rancors were not fully dissipated. In a general sense, and perhaps because of the maverick nature of Habib Bourguiba (who in this respect is like King Hussein of Jordan), Tunisia has never had any firm allies in the Arab world. In the 1960s it found itself at odds with practically everyone, especially President Nasser of Egypt.

In 1969 Colonel Qaddafi toppled a fusty, isolated monarchy; created a radical, Islamic republic; and thrust Libya to the center stage of Arab affairs. One of his first moves was to pull Libya out of the Maghreb and to put himself and his country at the disposal of Nasser's Egypt.[21] It is alleged that Boumedienne

---

[21] A good survey of modern Libya is G. Albergoni et al., *La Libye nouvelle: rupture et continuité*, CRESM (CNRS), Aix-en-Provence, 1975, especially Rémy Leveau, "Le système politique libyen," pp. 83–100.

chided him on this choice and prophesied that one day he would return to the Maghrebian fold. Steps toward unity with Egypt (and also the Sudan and Syria) did indeed fail, for several reasons: the death of Nasser; Libya's vitriolic hostility toward Egypt's emerging benefactor, King Faisal of Saudi Arabia; and President Sadat's misgivings about the Islamic cultural revolution Qaddafi was prescribing to remedy social ills.

Steps toward unity in the East having aborted definitely in September 1973, Libya turned to the West. In December 1973, after a meeting between Bourguiba and Qaddafi at Djerba, a project for Tunisian-Libyan unity was announced. The Tunisian elite had been inadequately prepared for this move, but just as important, Algeria let it be known that it disapproved of Tunisia's unilateral decision without prior consultation with its Maghrebi neighbors. The project simply fizzled out thereafter. Libya's isolation was such that it began a rapprochement with Morocco, although on two earlier occasions the Libyans had enthusiastically applauded the attempted overthrow of Morocco's king. After Algeria had been outmaneuvered by Morocco's "green march" into the Spanish Sahara, Boumedienne, with careful advance work, met with Qaddafi in Hassi Beida, Algeria. The Libyans altered their stance on the Sahara. They had initially argued that the essential objective was to liberate a piece of Arab territory, regardless of which Arabs were to control it. After Hassi Beida, the Libyans condemned the Moroccan-Mauritanian take-over and endorsed the principle of self-determination. It is believed that they also offered Algeria military support in the event of hostilities. In return, Boumedienne made references to the need for unity among progressive Arab regimes and left open the possibility that Algeria and Libya might have a future together.

The amount of attention paid here to the problems of Maghrebi unity, and especially Algeria's role in dealing with them, is warranted because Algeria has been the most active Arab state in Third World politics and North-South relations. Prior to the Sahara struggle, Boumedienne's regime had successfully built its reputation for seriousness and neutrality in intra-Arab disputes, and without excessive moralizing had moved other Arab states, in and out of OPEC, to an understanding of the major issues in the debate over a new world economic order. To cap it all, Algeria appeared to be on the path to achieving the kind of economic weight that would lend credence to its words.

But Boumedienne has put both his international stature and his economic strategy on the line in his confrontation with Morocco over the Sahara. Like Nasser in 1961, he has warned that integration among politically dissimilar regimes is impossible, but his sense of pique is shared by only a few other Arab states. Most have acknowledged Morocco's claims by their silence, while the Sudan and Tunisia have endorsed them publicly. Simultaneously, Algeria's relations have soured with Spain as well as with France, which has implicitly recognized Morocco's takeover by agreeing to sell arms to the monarchy.

Whatever the outcome of the Saharan dispute, Algeria seems likely to have great difficulty in recapturing its momentum and stature in the shaping of Third World policies toward the rich. As a party to an intense regional rivalry that will continue in one form or another into the 1980s, Algeria will lose the aura of lofty disinterestedness that it has carefully cultivated. Instead it will direct diplomatic efforts toward isolating and discrediting Morocco. On this basis we can hazard a middle-range forecast of Maghrebi development: Algerian hegemony will be thwarted throughout the 1980s. The EEC will be able, whenever convenient, to play a renascent Morocco against Algeria. The new Common Market accords, although of unlimited duration, are drafted separately for each of the North African states. It is unlikely that the accords will move the Maghrebi states closer together. As the Algerian diplomat Abdelqadar Chanderli wrote some years ago, "Preferences, whether tariff or structural, entail every possible political disadvantage and *work to increase the walling off of one developing country from another.*"[22]

Egypt, Libya, the Sudan

What will the Arabs do faced with the population increase in the Nile Valley from Khartoum to Alexandria, in an area they have outgrown

[22]In *The Atlantic Papers*, p. 70.

and continue to outgrow? Forty million people or something close to it in Egypt alone and perhaps twice that number by the year 2000. It is obvious that we would be committing a cardinal error if we were to treat this as a purely Egyptian problem. It is not merely an Egyptian problem but that, at least, of its immediate neighbors: Libya, the Sudan, Saudi Arabia, and Palestine. For its vital living space is narrow. There can be only two outcomes. Either this living space is expanded through modern technology, or the human pressure will explode in the form of migration and colonization outside the Nile Valley.[23]

Habib Bu al-'Aras

The "unity of the Nile" is a nationalist slogan that dates to Great Britain's de facto removal of the Sudan from the direct control of the Egyptian monarchy in the 1920s. Nationalists from Egypt, the downstream state, probably espoused this slogan with greater conviction than did their upstream neighbors, but there was a considerable body of Sudanese opinion that endorsed Egypto-Sudanese unity as well. In the early 1950s, after Nasser had come to power in Egypt and as the British were liquidating their position in the Middle East (except for Aden and the Gulf), it was widely assumed that the Sudan and Egypt would spontaneously merge once the British left. But between 1953, when the winding-down of the British presence began, and 1956, when the Sudan became formally independent, the momentum toward unity was lost. Many of those Sudanese deemed to be Egyptian allies made common cause with the Egyptians mainly to get the British out, not to bring the Egyptians in.[24]

In one important respect this failure to unify brought the Egyptians up short. Plans were already well advanced for the High Dam south of Aswan. If the Sudan and Egypt were to become one nation, there was no rush in working out the way Nile waters would be apportioned after the dam was operating. The allocation would be worked out not between two sovereign nation-states but within a unified political authority governing a single national (even if confederal) entity. The illusion of that

[23]Habib Bu al-'Aras, "The Foremost Arab Economic Need," *Al-Iqtisad al-Arabi*, no. 1, December 1974–January 1975, p. 13, in Arabic.
[24]See P. M. Holt, *A Modern History of the Sudan*, Weidenfeld and Nicolson, London, 1967, pp. 161–170.

possibility was dispelled in the minds of the Egyptians in 1955, after which hard negotiations led to the 1959 Nile Waters Agreement. This agreement is of more than passing interest, for it is almost unique among Arab states, setting down guidelines for the regulation of the use of the Nile's discharge and providing for a joint, permanent, technical commission and inspection stations to supervise implementation of the agreement. The formula has actually worked to the relative satisfaction of both parties for more than a decade since the Nile was first blocked at the dam site in 1964. It could be something of a model for the rest of the Arab world, particularly the states in the Tigris-Euphrates Valley.

From 1956 until 1969, there was very little talk of unity in the Nile Valley. In 1969, though, new and weak military regimes in both Libya and the Sudan looked to Nasserist Egypt for support and regional legitimation. The way was clear to consolidate what was known as the Federation of Arab Republics, which would have also included Syria, but the Sudan broke ranks. Since 1955, in fact, when resistance to union with Egypt had developed a critical mass within the Sudan, the three southern, non-Arab, largely non-Muslim provinces of the country had entered into various phases of armed resistance to northern dominance. The struggle became particularly violent and devastating after 1964, impeding the country's development as effectively as had the Kurdish revolt in Iraq. Colonel (now General) Ja'far Muhammad Numayri, who assumed control of the Sudan by a coup d'état in 1969, was the first Sudanese head of state (a northerner like all his predecessors) to have the wisdom and courage to seek accommodation with the south. This was laboriously achieved, through the good offices of Haile Selassie of Ethiopia, in 1972. Regional autonomy and a regional government were granted the south, and one of the implicit conditions of the settlement was that the Sudan would not immerse itself in any Arab unity scheme, one of whose effects would inevitably be to reduce the leverage within the country of the non-Arab south. Since 1972, it has become apparent that Numayri, unable to build any solid constituency among his fellow northerners, has entered into a kind of alliance with the south, whose leaders see in him the best deal they ever got from the north. The north would not be much without the south, which is amply endowed with tributaries of the White Nile, rainfall, forests, and savannahs, and which consequently has great agricultural potential. A truncated northern Sudan could be absorbed by Egypt, and on Egypt's terms. Thus the prospects are good for the continued existence of the present Sudanese state, and as long as both north and south value their own union there can be no further steps toward Arab unity. As noted earlier, even the agricultural development authority proposed by the Arab Fund for Economic and Social Development and endorsed by Khartoum may seem threatening in this respect.

Agricultural Hinterland

Nonetheless, the Arab world is growing infatuated with the Sudan as a potential provider of many of the agricultural products Arab states must now import from non-Arab states. The Arabian peninsula and its Gulf states, one of the region's most important food-deficit areas, is also its wealthiest. The geographical proximity of the Sudan to Saudi Arabia and to the peninsula as a whole suggests the sorts of exchanges possible between the two regions. The Sudan may become an agricultural hinterland for the oil-surplus states of the Arabian peninsula, which, in turn, can certainly fund the Sudan's agricultural modernization, a challenge that the indebted Egyptians cannot possibly face. Libya, some observers would argue, could bankroll the same projects in the name of the overall development of the subregion. But Libyan-Egyptian hostility and the inability of the Sudan, because of its southern regions, to intensify integration with its two northern neighbors make that alternative unrealistic.

Egypt is the largest importer of foodstuffs in the Middle East: 5 million tons of grains, fodder, edible oils, and meat were imported in 1976 at an estimated cost of £E 650 million ($1.6 billion). The Sudan, as we have already noted, might be able to cover Egypt's needs for sugar, edible oils, fodder, and beef in coming years. Conversely, Egypt's industries are far more advanced than those in the Sudan. Egypt could, through existing frame agreements, exchange its manufactures for the Sudan's agricultural produce. Further, Egypt has the surplus technology that the Sudan will require to develop its ports, roads, railroads, and vast agricultural schemes. Egypt may even entertain the hope that the Sudanese might one day welcome Egyptian peasants, whom the Sudanese willingly admit outperform their own, on a *permanent* basis.[25] For their part, the Sudanese are willing to contemplate the temporary importation of Egyptian labor—on which they relied in the past for dam building and land development—but they will not participate in population redistribution schemes.

The logic of Nile Valley economic integration perhaps appears so compelling to the Egyptians that they assume it will take place. Egypt and the Sudan both have officials of ministerial rank entrusted with promoting closer links. A number of joint projects have been developed on paper, the most important of which is the Jongeli Canal, which would drain part of the Sudd swamp and reduce the enormous losses of Nile waters that occur there each year through evaporation. Other paper projects include a beef and oil-seed scheme in the Blue Nile Damazin area and, more feasible, improvement of rail, road, and river transportation between the two countries. The problem is that all these projects are costly, and neither Egypt nor the Sudan has the foreign exchange to pay for them.

It may be the foreign exchange conundrum that will impede the development of these paper complementarities. The Sudan, no less than Egypt, has immediate needs for the importation of intermediate and capital goods (from diesel engines to irrigation pipes, tractors, turnkey sugar refineries, etc.) for development. The source of capital—and it will not be Egypt—will determine the development pattern. The Gulf area is now and will be in the foreseeable future the primary source of funding—whether

[25]Plans for resettling Egypt's surplus peasantry periodically resurface. Something of the kind was clearly envisaged during the union with Syria, 1958–1961, but never begun. Sudan's agricultural labor force is notoriously unstable and inefficient. If cultivation grows from 10 million to 30 million acres, who will do the farming? So far, however, only Iraq has set in operation plans to extend long-term tenancy to Egyptian peasants. A start was made with a pilot project for some 500 families in 1976.

through the AFESD, the Kuwait Fund for Arab Economic Development, the Saudi Arabian Monetary Agency, the Arab Investment Company, Gulf International, or others. While Egypt announces with great fanfare paper projects without visible funding for, say, cattle raising in the Damazin region between the Blue and White Niles, Gulf interests, capital in hand, are already moving into the same area. The London-based conglomerate Lonrho, Ltd., has raised Western and Gulf capital to promote a major sugar refinery at Kennana, which by 1980 should be exporting large amounts of refined sugar. Egypt could probably buy sugar by paying hard currency, but it would be very surprising if Egypt were able to work out a favorable barter agreement to exchange goods for sugar. The oil-seed, livestock, and fodder projects of the future may well follow the same pattern, with the Sudan selling abroad for hard currency rather than trading for Egyptian goods. Likewise, the Sudan is moving ahead in those manufacturing areas where Egypt should have comparative advantage. Gulf International and a few other companies will be able to meet domestic demand for textiles; even though their costs are high, they are protected by a high tariff wall. Foreign investors have been promised similar protection.[26] The one area of exchange Egypt will be able to pursue profitably is provision of highly trained Arabic-speaking labor, which it has in surplus.[27]

Saudi Arabia's Role

Crucial to any understanding of Egyptian-Sudanese-Libyan relations is the role of Saudi Arabia. By discussing it here, we are anticipating a more detailed treatment further on. Egypt and

[26]This takes us back to the futility of Arab free trade areas and the development of a common market. Both public and foreign-financed projects demand protection. Moreover, in the Sudan and other LDCs, high tariffs are an essential source of public revenues. See Ahmad Osman al-Hagg and Nagwa Ahmad al-Qadi, "The Experience of the Sudan in Planning with Regard to Arab Integration," Seminar on Long-Term Planning, p. 20.

[27]In 1974, the value of Egypt's exports to the Sudan was £E 5.2 million and the value of its imports was £E 7.1 million (total Egyptian exports in that year were valued at £E 587 million and imports at £E 909 million).

the Sudan are both Saudi clients but the reciprocal services demanded of them differ. Saudi Arabia's primary concern vis-à-vis Egypt is to keep it politically docile and, toward that end, to perpetuate its economic dependency. In respect to the Sudan, the objective is to build the land's agricultural potential in order to make the state both a source of supply for the peninsula and a profitable home for Saudi capital, public and private (the distinction is often hard to draw). It is not in the interests of Saudi Arabia to see the Sudan as a kind of agricultural hinterland to an industrializing Egypt. Nor, most emphatically, is it in the interests of Saudi Arabia to see Libya finance integration among the three countries. Such a development would lead inevitably to more radical regional policies on the part of Egypt and the Sudan, and conceivably, because of the Libyan will to self-annihilation, it might lead to Egypt's economic prosperity. This indeed might have been the course toward which Nasser was inching in 1969, but his successor, Anwar el-Sadat, could not feel comfortable with Qaddafi's radical puritanism. When Saudi Arabia indicated that it would be willing to offset any losses Egypt might incur by breaking off integral union with Libya (which was to have taken place September 1, 1973), Egypt complied.

Thus, instead of the creation of common capital, water, land, industry, and human resources among the original trio, there is instead a situation in which both the Sudan and Egypt are clients of a single patron, while Libya remains out in the cold.[28] It cannot be overstressed that what has been described as Saudi "policy" is a logical construct that emerges from an interpretation of Saudi actions. It may well be that there has been no conscious formulation of policy, but the implications of what is actually going on, no matter how improvised, lead in the direction described above.

The Sudan, banking on its agricultural potential, feels that it can eventually affirm its own economic sovereignty within this

[28]In 1974, the value of Egypt's exports to Libya was £E 9.8 million and the value of imports was £E 600,000. See the previous note for total import-export figures.

arrangement. That the Egyptians are also doggedly optimistic about their future requires much more explanation. Most Egyptians, regardless of their political outlook, believe that their country possesses the resources to become prosperous. In their view, the severe economic difficulties the country is facing are circumstantial, not structural. Their reasoning is shaped in part by a vision of Egypt's former role in the Arab world. First, it always was, and still is, the most populous of the Arab countries and the region's paramount military power. It was, moreover, an agriculturally rich country with abundant water and good soils. No other country could, nor yet does, rival Egyptian per-acre yields; today, however, no other country rivals Egypt's population density. Egypt was also the Arab world's industrial pioneer, from Mohammed Ali in the 1820s through the Misr Group of Talaat Harb and the state-owned schemes of the 1950s and 1960s, such as the Helwan Iron and Steel Company and Kima Fertilizers. The industrial base was expanded greatly between 1957 and 1965 but then stagnated as Egypt failed to develop much export capacity and hence could not muster the foreign exchange for further imports of capital goods and industrial raw materials. But the construction of the Aswan High Dam held out the promise of an abundant *domestic* source of hydroelectric energy and of the ability to absorb surplus population on reclaimed land. Finally, Egypt had the region's most extensive educational system, capped by three universities of international repute that offered quality instruction in all branches of engineering and medicine. In the early 1960s, it must have seemed to Nasser that Egypt was destined to be the major economic power of the Arab world. There were certainly, in those days of $2-a-barrel oil, no rivals in sight.

It is not surprising that contemporary Egyptian leadership still sees Egypt in that light. The "circumstantial" obstacles that derailed the Egyptian economy were the defeat of 1967, the mounting defense burden thereafter, and the direct and indirect costs of the 1973 war. Egyptian parliamentarians and officials have repeatedly pointed out that the country has sacrificed approximately $30 billion for the Arab cause in the last eight years, not to mention the thousands of dead in two wars and the devastation of three Canal-zone cities. They say the country needs a massive infusion of capital from the Arab "brethren" who benefited from the 1973 confrontation. And from this claim flows the notion of an Arab Marshall Plan to rebuild the economies of the front-line states. There is an implicit threat in this idea. Poor or destitute, Egypt will still have a big army and an important if dilapidated economic structure to support it. If the Arab rich choose to intensify Egypt's poverty, they risk seeing the overthrow of a moderate regime, perhaps the outbreak of a mass-based revolution, or at least the emergence of a military regime with Qaddafite proclivities. Nasser thought he could get his way with the Arab world by exploiting Egypt's strength; Sadat may believe he can have his way by exploiting Egypt's weakness.

Prospects for Egypt

Egypt needs but does not really want integration with other Arab states. Since the advent of Sadat, emphasis in the press and in public utterances has been upon "Egypt first." The populace has been told again and again how much it has sacrificed for the Arabs—the unstated conclusion being that it has done its duty. Surely the so-called rejection front among the Arabs and Palestinians has read this message clearly, despite Egypt's public remonstrances to the contrary. If Egypt-firstism is to succeed, however, it will require Egypt's close interaction with other Arab states over the short and the long term. The immediate need is for capital to pay for food imports, to service the debt, to overcome idle capacities in industry, and to rebuild the Canal zone. These measures, planners in Cairo hope, will put the economy back on its feet. Then Egypt will need regional markets for its surplus labor and its manufactures. Although they do not spell out how this scenario will be implemented, Egyptians do believe that it is feasible.

There are several good reasons to believe that Egypt's circumstantial bottlenecks have taken on such proportions that they have become quasi-structural. Let us move all too rapidly through them. Egypt's population in 1976 was 38 million and is likely to reach 70 million by the year 2000.[29] It might be possible, but at a very high cost and subject to constraints in water supply, to increase Egypt's cultivated surface by about 20 percent. The increase would consist of inferior desert soils, however. Even if accomplished, this effort would do little to mitigate growing population densities, which are compounded by annual net losses to urban expansion of 20,000 to 60,000 acres of good land. Egyptian planners must therefore think of moving 20 to 30 million Egyptians from currently inhabited areas to the western New Valley, the Red Sea, the northwest coast, Sinai, and the Canal zone (if not to neighboring Arab countries) over the next 25 to 50 years. No one really knows if this can be done, much less financed, but the problem obviously goes well beyond the circumstantial.

The development of industry and industrial exports is a partial response to overcrowding, population redistribution, and the need to finance future growth.[30] The task will not be any easier because it has already begun. Egypt's industrial base is older and more in need of technological overhaul than the industrial bases of wealthy industrial upstarts like Algeria or Iraq. All of the oil producers are expanding into industrial areas—textiles, iron and steel, cement, petrochemicals and fertilizers, automobile assembly—and using the latest technology. That Egypt finds itself importing Mercedes Benz buses from Iran when it has had its own assembly for 15 years is indicative of its dilemma. The industrial development in neighboring states poses the question of where Egypt will find regional markets for its industrial goods, even if it can revitalize its own industrial base. The situation is further complicated by 20 to 30 percent redundancy in public

[29]See John Waterbury, "Chickens and Eggs: Egypt's Population Explosion Revisited," *AUFS Report*, Northeast Africa Series, vol. 20, no. 1, 1975; and Nadir Fergany, "Prospects of Long-range Population Growth and Some Related Characteristics in Egypt," Seminar on Long-Term Planning.

[30]A sanguine analysis of how Egypt can achieve a per capita GNP of $1,000 by the year 2000 based on the conversion of a domestic dissavings rate to one of 20 percent per year of GNP, plus rapid industrial expansion in production and exports, is presented by Dr. Essam Muntaser, "Egypt's Long-Range Growth, 1976–2000: Preliminary Projections," ibid.

sector personnel and labor, low wage levels that have nonetheless risen more rapidly than production, and an administered price system that makes accurate cost accounting nearly impossible. There are hopes for increased oil production (50 million tons per year by 1980) and substantial foreign exchange revenues from the Suez Canal, tourism, and foreign investment. But these revenues must be put in the perspective of a current import bill on the order of $4 billion, i.e., about half the value of the gross domestic product (GDP); if Egypt's economy is to grow and its population is be fed, that bill undoubtedly will increase.

For nearly 30 years, Egypt's leaders have lived with one dominant reality and one overriding concern: conduct of the confrontation with Israel. That preoccupation is as strong today as ever, although President Sadat has demonstrated dramatically his desire to achieve a lasting settlement. For the time being, it is difficult to generate a concerted approach to the country's economic problems. It is easier, in the absence of a settlement with Israel, to tinker with the economy, to cajole or frighten foreign exchange support from regional and extraregional sources, and to rely on the Egyptians' 8,000 years of experience in dealing with the Nile Valley to provide a solution.

Future relations among Libya, Egypt, and the Sudan will hinge upon regime changes or their absence more than upon any other single factor. President Numayri has so far shown himself to be the most vulnerable of the national leaders, although given Qaddafi's personal anti-institutional style it is impossible not to question his longevity. Sadat may be less vulnerable than the others if his economy can be made to work, but it is moot whether or not he will succeed himself after his second mandate terminates in 1982.

After the attempted coup against Numayri in July 1976, Egypt more than ever became the military guarantor, and Saudi Arabia and Kuwait the financial guarantors, of the Sudan's regime. This puts Egypt in the odd position of helping to police the Sudan to protect Gulf and peninsula investments. The arrangement could continue as long as the southern Sudan does not feel it is being overwhelmed by outside Arab funds and arms, and Egypt develops no major conflict of interest with Saudi Arabia directly, or with Arab growth policies in the Sudan.

By contrast, the following would be a not unreasonable set of developments: In the early 1980s Egypt may discover that the level of Arab funding of its economy, as well as the International Monetary Fund (IMF) stabilization program endorsed in 1976 as a prerequisite for further Arab aid, have been insufficient to generate the rate of growth necessary to improve or even to hold steady the standard of living of the mass of Egyptians. On the one hand, Egypt would be driven to seek preferential deals with the Sudan on agricultural commodity imports against exports of manufactured goods, which the Sudan, guided by the preoccupations of Arab investors with getting maximum returns, might well deny. On the other hand, Egypt might be driven to adopt more aggressive postures vis-à-vis its Arab benefactors in order to wring more funds from them. If this aggressiveness was accompanied by a regime change in Egypt—peaceful or otherwise—the Cairo-Riyadh axis would be placed in serious jeopardy. A poorer and more militant Egypt would likely try to subjugate the Sudan and sabotage the Saudi regime. Saudi Arabia and the United States are well aware of this possibility and will aim to keep Egypt moderate and financially afloat, but dependent on their aid.

Saudi Arabia and the Gulf

At the risk of vexing you, I must maintain that we are still a poor country. Not only do we lack industry, agriculture; worse still, we lack manpower. We make our young people study and we send them to foreign universities, but it takes years to obtain a degree or a technical diploma. Meanwhile we have to import engineers, technicians, specialized workers that we don't know where to house because we lack hotels. To build hotels we need contractors, but the contractors themselves need hotels to live in. It's a vicious circle that exhausts us. Among other things we lack cement. We lack harbors because we lack the cement to build them. Last, but by no means least, we lack water. We haven't a single river, a single lake. We depend on rainfall alone.

For 100 years, it has rained less and less frequently, for the last 25 hardly at all.[31]

Sheikh Ahmed Zaki Yamani

It is hard to square this picture of poverty with Saudi Arabia's billions of dollars in oil earnings ($27.5 billion in 1974). Any of Saudi Arabia's problems can be solved, after a fashion, with money. Seawater can be desalinated, cement imported while cement factories are built, and labor and technological personnel recruited from the neighboring states and the world at large. Saudi Arabia can pay for just about anything; indeed, over the next five years, it is planning to do just that. Hisham Nazer, Minister of State for Planning, announced in May 1975 a $150 billion five-year development plan. Although this figure has subsequently been reduced to more modest proportions, Saudi Arabia still may try to invest annually funds worth more than double Egypt's current GNP. In addition to human resource development, vocational training, and the expansion of social services, the plan is to include water projects worth $11 billion, which should increase the production of desalinated water from 57 million to 163 million gallons per day; agricultural investments worth $1.3 billion; and expansion of electrical output worth $2 billion.

The bulk of the investment will go toward the development of infrastructure and industry. Saudi Arabia is aiming at supplying 11 percent of the world market for liquid petroleum gas (LPG) by the early 1980s. Two gas-gathering projects of primary importance will be supplemented by a fleet of LPG tankers. At least one steel mill having an initial annual capacity of 1.2 million tons and a plant to produce annually 1 million tons of nitrogenous fertilizers will be built. Aluminum mills, truck and car assemblies, and flour and feed mills are to follow. New industrial cities—notably Jubail on the Gulf—military complexes, and airports will also be constructed. As mentioned, it is unlikely that these projects will come about on the scale initially projected. Both Northern demand for petroleum and the OPEC price will increase in

[31]From an interview with Oriana Fallaci, "A Sheik Who Hates to Gamble," *New York Times Magazine*, September 14, 1975.

the next five years, but the real purchasing power of foreign exchange earnings may remain stagnant. Also, given the administrative and infrastructural backwardness of the country, it is difficult to imagine how such vast sums could actually be disbursed. But whatever the margin of error, Saudi Arabia will pay a fabulous price for its development. Its determination to do so reflects not economic sense but the regime's conviction of its mission to create a viable modern Islamic state. For Syrians and Egyptians, among others, logic would indicate massive capital transfers to a place where infrastructure, human resources, industrial base, and local markets already exist. Starting from scratch in a waterless desert is seen for its very lack of economic justification as an "irresponsible" waste of what should be considered a regional resource.[32] And in that wastage, Saudi Arabia risks undermining the unique opportunity the oil-less, capital-starved states of the area have to break out of their underdevelopment.

Beyond this, one must ponder the likely social and political consequences of this development strategy within Saudi society. Most of the Saudi population has not been involved, in an occupational sense, in the oil boom. Social services, education, and money have trickled down to the Bedouin. The service of some people in the army has exposed them to the paraphernalia of a modern state. The real Saudi participants in the oil-based economy have been the small royal and urban bourgeois elites that make up the highest echelons of the government apparatus, the officers' corps, and the small (but rich) trading and business sector. The oil industry itself is not a big employer, and the market for unskilled and semiskilled labor has been filled mostly by Omanis and Yemenis, not Saudis. Of the estimated 50,000 people employed in industry, more than half are foreign and 60 percent are illiterate. Current estimates are that Saudi Arabia

[32]Dow Chemical is working out an accord with Petromin of Saudi Arabia for a petrochemical complex that will produce, among other things, 450,000–500,000 tons of ethylene per year. Cost estimates are $1 billion, which is 50 percent more than the building costs in an industrialized country. See "Petrochimie: où en sont les projets?" *Economia* (France), no. 18, December 1975, pp. 53–64.

will have to import some 300,000 workers, not including an additional 25,000 managers and technicians, over the next five years.[33] The Saudi Arabia of the future could take on a peculiar socioeconomic configuration, with a mandarinate of the Wahhabi sect—the puritanical Islamic sect from which the reigning dynasty is derived—controlling policymaking and supervising highly skilled foreign personnel in two key areas: managing oil revenues and investment and executing projects to strengthen industry and infrastructures. The middle-range managerial personnel and skilled and semiskilled workers throughout the modern sector would be just as likely, if not more so, to be foreign as Saudi. With the exception of the commercial and governmental elites, most Saudis might be only marginally involved onlookers to the transformation of their society. It would, in short, be a challenge for the mandarinate to retain control over the system they hope to create.

For the late King Faisal (who was assassinated in April 1975), there was nothing illogical or irresponsible about Saudi development plans. He had a mission, as do Boumedienne and now King Khalid (and, more significantly, Prince Fahd). It is one directed first to the Arab world but, in general, to Muslims everywhere. The goal is to create a prosperous, educated society, drawing its livelihood from heavy industry and advanced technology while retaining as an ideology and guide to conduct the core of puritan Wahhabi Islam. Faisal first publicized this mission in 1965 when he called for an "Islamic Alliance." Tunisia's Habib Bourguiba, of all people, expressed interest in the alliance, but it was roundly denounced by Nasser as an imperialist ploy to divide the Arabs. Even conservative Arab regimes remained cautiously aloof from Faisal's alliance, but isolation was nothing new to the monarchy.

Geographic and political isolation is a fact of recent Saudi history. Socialist, or at least radical, Egypt was a clear threat

[33]"Work Opportunities in the Arab Oil-Producing Countries," *Arab Business*, no. 2, February–March 1976, pp. 8–9, in Arabic. A detailed study of Saudi plans has been presented by Dr. Hasim Khawajika, "Aspects of Saudi Arabia's Economic Growth," *Journal of Gulf and Arabian Peninsula Studies*, vol. 2, no. 5, January 1976, pp. 173–187.

to both the Saudi regime and its principal source of wealth. Hashemite Jordan, and until 1958 Hashemite Iraq, were as conservative and pro-Western in their policies as the Saudis; but because it was the Hashemite family that the House of Saud had driven from the peninsula after World War I, relations were uneasy. Cordial relations with Iran were difficult because of the profound cleavage between Shi'ite and Wahhabite Islam, a factor that played and still plays an equally important role in relations with Iba dite Oman and the Zaydi Imams of Yemen (both the Ibadis and Zaydis being Shi'ite subsects). Saudi Arabia's one staunch friend and undeclared ally over the last 40 years has been the United States. It is beyond the scope of this study to explore the relationship in any detail, but it is important to emphasize that the United States interest has been based on considerations of assured energy supplies for the "free world" and, subsequently, of the business health of the United States oil industry. As a result of that interest the United States has attempted to thwart any steps toward the absorption of Saudi Arabia into any unity scheme. It was on the basis of both these considerations that Nasser was seen as such a threat when he advocated integral union. This was particularly the case between 1962 and 1967, when Egyptian forces were heavily involved in the Yemeni civil war. Both Saudi Arabia and the United States came to believe that the Egyptian presence in the southwest corner of the Arabian peninsula was but the prelude to a subversive effort on the part of Egypt to topple the Saudi regime and somehow "grab" the peninsula's oil. For their part, radical Arab regimes saw the United States (and, by extension, Israel) as the principal impediment to a rational utilization of Arab resources. The scenario is a microcosm of North-South relations today, except that the confrontation in the 1950s and 1960s was expressed in cold war, geopolitical terms.

The turning point in Saudi Arabia's regional stature came at the Khartoum Conference of August 1967, which was convened to discuss Arab strategy in light of the recent Israeli victory. With the Egyptian army and economy in ruins, Nasser had to accept annual subsidies (totaling £110 million per year) from Saudi Arabia, Kuwait, and Libya to compensate Egypt for the loss of tourism, Canal traffic, and oil resulting from the defeat. Egypt's armies had left Yemen forever during the June war. Egypt had taken the first step toward clientage with the Saudis, but another patron, the Soviet Union, provided an ample counterweight to growing Saudi influence. Reconciliation between Egypt and Saudi Arabia was unlikely during Nasser's lifetime, but after his death in September 1970 a new warmth in Saudi-Egyptian relations quickly developed. Sadat may have felt that a strategy of accommodation and friendship would be more effective in putting Saudi and other Arab oil earnings to work for the Egyptians than Nasser's strategy of threats, confrontation, and subversion. He may well have been correct: Saudi Arabia and the Gulf states have channeled considerable amounts of aid and credits to Egypt, above all since 1973. Saudi Arabia, Kuwait, and Jordan, all of which had maintained relations with the United States after 1967, began to serve as emissaries in the slow reestablishment of normal relations between Egypt and the United States beginning in 1971. Both the expulsion of Soviet military missions from Egypt in 1972 and the inauguration of the open-door policy to attract foreign private capital to the Egyptian economy are partially due to Saudi advice that these moves would be conducive to Saudi assistance to Egypt, and that the United States would also look favorably on either move.

One of the costs to Egypt of reconciliation with Saudi Arabia was, as we have seen, the alienation, however temporary, of Libya. A potentially far greater cost exists in the likely nature of Saudi Arabia's medium- and long-term objectives. Here again the interpretation of a "policy" may be more a logical construct than a coherent program of action. After more than a decade of bitter confrontation with Egypt, Saudi Arabia found itself with considerable control over Egypt's financial solvency and economic well-being because Egypt was and is economically weak. Saudi Arabia, a regime that had been on the defensive during the 1960s, was rather abruptly in the driver's seat; more than that, it enhanced its own regional weight by having as a dependent a country of the importance of Egypt. The relationship as it now stands could hardly be improved upon—as the Saudis see it—

unless it were to give Saudi capital greater access to the Egyptian market. But the perpetuation of this *rapport de forces* is contingent upon Egypt's remaining economically weak. Hard-nosed national self-interest would dictate that Saudi Arabia aid Egypt only to the extent of staving off economic collapse, but never enough to permit it to cut the umbilical cord to the Saudi treasury. Dependency links usually are underscored by substantial reliance upon bilateral credits and aid, which have constituted the major form of Saudi assistance to Egypt.[34] Nonetheless, after Egypt announced its acceptance in principle of an IMF stabilization plan in the spring of 1976, Saudi Arabia took a 40 percent interest in a $2 billion fund to aid the Egyptian economy on a strictly businesslike basis. Sadat publicly declared this level of funding to be far below Egypt's real needs, but even so the Gulf Organization for the Development of Egypt (Kuwait, Qatar, and the United Arab Emirates are the other subscribers) may establish a lien on the Egyptian economy and an influence on growth strategies similar to that of AFESD in the Sudan. In other words, basic decisions affecting the growth of the Nile Valley may now be taken in Washington, D.C., Riyadh, and Kuwait.

In the two-tiered economic hierarchy of the Middle East, Saudi Arabia is an actual or potential patron for the oil-less. At the same time, it is a partner of and regional broker for Northern business interests, foremost among them those of the United States. It is by now common knowledge that Lockheed and other corporations have found profitable markets there and have rewarded their local brokers handsomely. Corporate America is ubiquitous in Saudi Arabia. Aramco was the pioneer, but now many other giants have entered the field with dazzling development plans on the drawing boards. The United States is Saudi Arabia's major supplier, but interests as diverse as the Stanford

[34]From October 1973 through December 1975 Saudi Arabia loaned or granted Egypt about $2 billion. The last soft loan of $600 million in the late spring of 1975 was used to pay off short-term debt. Saudi Arabia does participate in multilateral schemes such as AFESD, the Kuwait Fund, the Arab Investment Company, and the Arab Navigation Company for oil tankers (the latter is sponsored by the Organization of Arab Petroleum Exporting Countries).

Research Institute, Arthur D. Little, Inc., and the Army Corps of Engineers are advising the Saudis on various projects. Further, Saudi Arabia purchased over $120 million in food products from the United States in 1975, a sum scheduled to rise to $200 million in 1976. This, not incidentally, is the kind of business that Saudi Arabia could offer the Sudan. One United States project, joining together the sublime and ridiculous in Saudi development, is an air-conditioned feedlot station in the Hofuf area. In sum, Saudi Arabia has become not only a vital market for United States goods and know-how, but also a major holder of United States bonds and securities. In 1975 the Saudi Arabian Monetary Agency was estimated to hold $9 billion in United States government bonds and securities and another $1 billion in corporate stocks and bonds. The Saudi connection, then, is almost as special to the United States as that between the United States and Israel. One must logically expect that the United States will spare no effort in safeguarding that relationship, especially if a threat of a change in regimes arises.

Saudi Arabia's major rivals to the east are Iraq and Iran. Financially independent and adhering to a militant Arabist ideology, Iraq could pose the same kind of threat to the monarchy as did Nasser in an earlier era. By contrast, there is a tacit if uneasy entente with conservative, expansionist, and Shi'ite Iran. Caught among these relative giants are the Gulf states—Kuwait, Bahrain, Qatar, the United Arab Emirates, Oman—and also the two Yemens.

In 1961, when General Abdulkrim Qassim of Iraq threatened to absorb Kuwait, not only the British but also Egypt and Saudi Arabia headed off the move. For these countries, the prospect of Iraq controlling Kuwait's large oil reserves meant the upsetting of the regional balance of power. That, at least, was Egypt's major concern, while Saudi Arabia was apprehensive that newly republican and politically radical Iraq would aim next at the House of Saud. Kuwait narrowly escaped with and was able to consolidate its independence as Baghdad became enmeshed in semiconstant warfare with the Kurds of northern Iraq.

Kuwait, sensing that its regional vulnerability arose from its dwarf size and "indecent" wealth, went about making itself "worthwhile" to other Arab states, principally through the Kuwait Fund for Arab Economic Development (currently capitalized at $3.4 billion). In the final analysis, the Kuwaitis as much as the Saudis will survive and thrive in an Arab world of states whose interests often conflict. It is in this sense that both Kuwait and Saudi Arabia frequently are suspected of perpetuating the Arab-Israeli conflict and the nonsettlement of the Palestinian question because those problems so consistently divide the major Arab military powers. Influence and survival for the oil-rich mini-states lie in the interstices of regional cleavages. At the same time the Arab-Israeli dispute, the Palestinian issue, and glaring gaps in the distribution of wealth sharpen the focus and demands of radical forces within the Arab world. It requires very agile diplomacy to balance the immediate benefits and potential costs of regional fragmentation, but the Kuwaitis, particularly in their relations with the Palestinians, have become masters at it.

The Kuwaitis have loaned or advanced credits to Egypt worth more than $1.5 billion since October 1973. They cannot make Egypt a client, but they can make themselves sufficiently valuable to the Egyptians so that Cairo would block any Iraqi or Saudi move toward the absorption of Kuwait. The same considerations guide Kuwait's relations with Syria. In this sense, the Kuwaitis have an interest in a moderate, but economically strong, Egypt and Syria, whereas Saudi Arabia wants those states to be politically docile.

Kuwait society is already the peculiar hybrid that Saudi Arabia may one day become—although Kuwait lacks Saudi Arabia's industrial potential. Two-thirds of the 350,000 persons in the work force are non-Kuwaitis. In primary and secondary education, 90 percent of the personnel is foreign. In the next few years Kuwait will probably need to import another 50,000 foreign workers. Among the foreign personnel are more than 40,000 Palestinians, many of whom first entered Kuwait after 1948 when the country was still poor, but who now occupy important posts throughout the state apparatus. Yassir Arafat first brought together the nucleus of what was to become al-Fatah among the

Palestinian diaspora in Kuwait, and the regime has given financial aid to al-Fatah and the Palestine Liberation Organization (PLO) since 1967. Nonetheless, Palestinians, like all other foreigners, mix with native Kuwaitis only through their work. In most other respects Kuwaitis and non-Kuwaitis form two separate societies.

Much the same pattern is repeating itself throughout the Emirates on the Arab shores of the Gulf. The Bahrainis see their future in offshore banking, perhaps even as the financial center that Beirut once was. Abu Dhabi, Qatar, Dubai, Sharjah, and Oman all are developing small but technologically advanced armies as well as nascent refining and petrochemical industries and booming cities that move goods and capital. Abu Dhabi, through its own development fund, is following Kuwait's path to regional acceptance. Added to the expatriate Arab work force found elsewhere are large numbers of Iranians, Pakistanis, and Indians in the work forces of Qatar, Oman, and the United Arab Emirates. To preserve their independence, these states must hope for a sort of Iranian–Saudi Arabian condominium over the Gulf that would tolerate their presence.

Iran and Saudi Arabia are about equally concerned with the Dhofar liberation movement backed by South Yemen. The guerrilla movement operating in the Dhofar province of the Sultanate of Oman poses the same threat (on a much smaller scale) as did Nasser's intervention in North Yemen. Saudi Arabia would like to see the liberation movement snuffed out and the regime in South Yemen domesticated or replaced. Iran, for its part, would not tolerate a radical regime in Oman at the entrance to the Gulf. South Yemen is for the moment extremely isolated, and Iranian and Omani troops, with Jordanian support, have been able to contain the front. Earlier, Kuwait and some Gulf Emirates extended aid to South Yemen, whose economy, totally dependent upon the port of Aden, stagnated during the eight years in which the Suez Canal was closed. (As a result, the Popular Front for the Liberation of the Gulf and Oman has been obliged to drop "Gulf" from its title.) Saudi Arabia has now offered South Yemen $400 million to help finance its development plan. Strengthening the Saudi squeeze on the Adeni regime are the reported negotiations for unity between North Yemen and Saudi Arabia in the fields of defense, foreign policy, and culture.[35]

Assuming the survival of the Saudi and Egyptian regimes, the 1980s will witness the institutionalization of the financial dependency that has increasingly marked relations between the two countries since 1967. With Egypt being politically neutralized and Iran sympathetic to the containment of any radical regimes on the Arabian peninsula, Saudi Arabia can become co-guarantor of the status quo in that area. But the neutrality, if not the friendliness, of Egypt is absolutely requisite to Saudi predominance. An unfriendly Egypt, as existed throughout the 1960s, could attack Riyadh through the mini-states along the Saudi periphery. By contrast, because Iran is a non-Arab, non–Sunni Muslim country, even a change in its regime or policies would not have the same potential for reversing alliances as a re-radicalized Egypt.

The Fertile Crescent

The two protagonists in the subregion of the Fertile Crescent are Iraq and Syria, whose relations were aptly summarized by *The Economist*: "Iraq and Syria are neighborly 'sister' Arab countries divided by a common Baathist ideology and a common river, the Euphrates."[36] Every logical reason for uniting drives these two regimes further apart. The nub of the problem is that the two countries, whose official, constitutional credo is to pursue Arab unity within a Baathi socialist framework, are governed by different wings of the mother party. Perhaps the conflicts reflect some atavistic rivalry between "upstream" and "downstream" interests, but in their intensity they go far beyond any tensions between Egypt and the Sudan.

[35]*Ruz al-Yussef*, February 1, 1976, carried the report on unity negotiations. On the Dhofar front and South Yemen, see Fred Halliday, *Arabia Without Sultans: A Political Survey of Instability in the Arab World*, Vintage Books, New York, 1975, and Philippe Rondot, "Le sultanat d'Oman devant le rébellion de Dhofar," *Maghreb-Machrek*, no. 70, October–December 1975, pp. 38–46.

[36]"Sisterly Spite," *The Economist*, April 26, 1975, p. 67.

The latter hypothesis is the more convincing in view of the difficulty of discerning any real ideological difference between the once-radical Baathists of Damascus and the conservative (perhaps nonideological) Baathists of Baghdad. When identifiably extreme Baathists came to power in Syria in 1966 and some of the more moderate ones fled to Beirut and Baghdad, there was a discernible ideological gap. But since Hafez al-Assad asserted his control over Syria in November 1970, the justification for the ideological contention has vanished. Socialism, Arabism, unity, anti-Zionism, restoration of Palestinian rights, and political hostility toward the United States are the basic common interests of the two factions. Both maintain good relations with the Soviet Union, which is in turn their major source of arms. Since 1973 they have, like Algeria before them, developed economic exchanges with France and, more significantly, with the United States. They accept the Algerian distinction between foreign policy goals and economic self-interest. What keeps Iraq and Syria at each other's throat, then, is something far more, or far less, than ideology.

Iraq may well see its future in the Fertile Crescent much as Algeria pictures its own in the Maghreb. It is allocating $3 billion a year to accelerate its development and is out to buy the best technology the (Western) world can provide.[37] It does not for the moment harbor designs against the territorial integrity of Kuwait, but it is most interested in making adjustments along the Shatt al-Arab—a river that forms part of the Iraqi-Iranian border—and the border with Kuwait that would allow it to develop a deepwater port at the head of the Gulf. It has entered into the aid-granting game and has established the Iraqi Fund for External Development (capitalized at $170 million). It may, moreover, be "floating" on oil reserves second only to those of Saudi Arabia. In February 1975, Vice President Saddam Hussein announced that Iraq would produce an annual surplus of 30 million tons of crude oil in order to use the proceeds for aid to

[37]"Banking and Finance in Iraq," *Africa/Middle East Business Digest*, March 1975, pp. 17–19.

Arab and other developing nations. Directly affecting relations with Syria has been the construction of a pipeline from the northern oil fields to the head of the Gulf. Iraq can now pump its oil out of the country without having to use existing pipelines to the Mediterranean that pass through Syria. At the same time, according to an agreement of 1972, Iraq has supplied crude oil to Syria at $2.30 per barrel.[38]

Syria's wealth is not as dazzling as that of Iraq, but it could be formidable. Syria, too, holds trump cards of its own. Having nearly doubled its oil production since 1974, reaching 210,000 barrels per day (bpd), Syria stands to earn $500 million from oil exports. Its agricultural and agro-industrial future is bright, especially now that the Soviet-built Tabaqa Dam on the Euphrates has been completed. This project will bring irrigation water and hydroelectric power to large areas of the Jazira area in eastern Syria. But it was executed without Syria's having reached any prior accord with Iraq on the apportionment of the water of the Euphrates after the dam's construction. In the spring of 1975, a major crisis between the two countries developed when Iraq claimed, with apparent justification, that it was receiving about 40 percent less water than it needed for its own agriculture. Saudi Arabia stepped in as the honest broker and tried to move the two Baathi leaderships toward some sort of accord.

Iraq, a bona fide member of the "rejection front" (bringing it in alignment with Libya in this respect), does not border Israel, nor is any of its territory occupied by Israel. Its staunch refusal to condone any dealings with the Israelis until Palestinian rights are fully restored is nearly costless. Above all, the proclaimed purity of the Iraqis on this issue is constantly measured against the position of their Baathi brethren in Syria. Syria does border Israel, which also occupies some of its territory. Hafez al-Assad can ill afford the luxury of intransigence for long, but all his

[38]"An Interview with Comrade Adnan Hamdani Regarding the Strategy of Oil Policy," *Petroleum and Development*, vol. 1, no. 2, December 1975, pp. 21–33, in Arabic. After the Syrian "invasion" of Lebanon, Iraq stopped pumping oil through the Banyas (Syria) terminal, causing Syria to revise downward its projected investment outlays.

moves, and many he has never contemplated, are given full publicity by the Iraqis. In addition, the second disengagement agreement between Israel and Egypt of September 1975 left Syria in a singularly exposed position. The portent of Egypt's acceptance of nonbelligerency pledges was to leave Syria nearly alone to face the Israelis on the northern Golan front. Iraq did not leave Syria in peace as it sought a nonsuicidal way out of its predicament.

Syria clearly felt its isolation and military exposure, both of which have been compounded by its direct involvement in the Lebanese cockpit. Syria's aims are probably twofold: first, to emasculate the Palestinian resistance so as to be able to move toward disengagement talks of its own; second, to create a little "Greater Syria" in which Damascus would be the center of gravity for a reconstituted (or partitioned) Lebanon, a quasi-client state in Jordan, and the remnants of the Palestinian movement, whether or not anchored to a West Bank state.[39] This would indeed make Syria a most credible counterweight to Iraq and even to Egypt. The goal is attainable, especially in that it had, at least in its initial phases, the tacit backing of the United States and Israel, but it leaves Assad indecently exposed as a minoritarian ('Alwite) leader in league with Christian zealots and Arab reactionaries against the guerrillas. Many Arab heads of state may be privately happy with Syria's throttling of the Palestinians, but few refrained from denouncing Syria as a traitor. However, with a semblance of order restored in Lebanon in the fall of 1976, the continued presence of a Syrian "dissuasion force" in that country was agreed upon by moderate Arab regimes led by Saudi Arabia and including Egypt.

Jordan has felt as isolated as Syria as a result of the second disengagement and even more so as a result of the resolution of the Arab heads of state at Rabat in 1974 that only the PLO can

[39]At the end of 1975 there was some breakdown in the coalition between the Syrian Baath and the Syrian Communist parties. It is believed that the latter questioned the rapprochement with Jordan, President Assad's state visit to Iran, and an alleged request to Washington for food aid. Syria has received about $800 million from Saudi Arabia and Kuwait since the end of 1973.

legitimately speak in the name of the Palestinians. The resolution, in effect, denied Jordan any further rights to the West Bank. King Hussein sensed an opportunity to make Jordan's weight felt once again as progress toward military coordination with Syria quickened. He reconvened the Jordanian parliament, which was elected in 1966 and dissolved in 1974, seating 30 representatives from the Palestinian West Bank. The PLO, Egypt, and others have denounced the move as a flagrant violation of the Rabat resolution. Syria and the leader of al-Sa'iqa, the Syrian-sponsored Palestinian guerrilla group, professed not to understand the reason for all the fuss. The trade-off is that Syria will acknowledge a Jordanian role in determining the fate of the West Bank in exchange for Jordan's implicit acceptance of Syrian preeminence in the western Fertile Crescent. It is likely that Hashemite Jordan regards its current alliance with Syria as no more than tactical. Geopolitical considerations in this instance have left all the states of the Fertile Crescent in disarray, and Saudi Arabia prodding all parties toward moderate positions on the Israeli question. More than any other subregion, the Fertile Crescent has seen the world through the prism of the confrontation with Israel and the question of Palestinian nationhood. It has consequently proven unable to focus consistently on problems of regional development and resource allocation that are equally, if not more, significant.

Like the Maghreb, the Fertile Crescent is a promising economic region whose constituent states have assiduously abetted its continued disunity. While it is possible that either the Syrian or Iraqi Baath party might be able to engineer a change of regimes in the other country favorable to itself, there is little reason to expect that the Fertile Crescent will form a cohesive unit during the 1980s. To the contrary, at least two neighbors, Iran and Saudi Arabia, have an interest in keeping this cauldron simmering. Added to their interest is the fact that in one form or another, the Arab-Israeli dispute and the remaking of Lebanon will affect relations among states in the region during the next decade. The status quo in the Gulf area and on the peninsula may be seen by its backers as a function of continued disarray in the Fertile Crescent.

Iran

The Pahlavi dynasty has every intention of making Iran the dominant economic and military power in the Northern tier, in the Fertile Crescent, and on the Arabian peninsula including its Gulf states; it also intends to make Iran an equal to India in control of the Indian Ocean. The prospects that Iran will fulfill its ambitions are good. If it succeeds in the process it will become a world power. To support these ambitions the country has not only its inherent strengths but also the structural or circumstantial weakness of all its neighbors, save one. The exception, of course, is the Soviet Union, which borders Iran for 1,500 miles.

Iran's inherent strengths lie in its large domestic market, agricultural potential, supply of water and power, abundant natural resources (especially oil and natural gas), and relatively large number of high-level managerial and technocratic personnel. Added to these are the armed forces, which are equipped largely with United States materiel that many NATO allies would envy. The Iranian navy is without equal in the Gulf and must now be taken as a force to be reckoned with in the Indian Ocean. The strength of the Iranian navy suggests the heart of Iran's regional strategy—to be in military control of physical access to the world's largest cluster of oil reserves. Currently the Arabian peninsula and its Gulf states, plus Iraq and Iran, hold about 55 percent of the world's proven reserves (see Table 2). Although the recent increases in the estimates of the reserves of China, Iraq, and Mexico show that this figure can vary fairly widely, the Gulf is almost certain to remain the single most vital oil-bearing region in the world for the rest of the century. According to the Exxon Corporation, the world is currently consuming the equivalent of 85 million bpd to generate energy, of which 55 percent actually is oil, 18 percent coal, 20 percent gas, 6 percent hydroelectric, and 1 percent nuclear power. By 1990, total energy consumption will have risen to the equivalent of 160 million bpd, of which 49 percent will be oil, 17 percent coal, 12 percent nuclear power, and the remaining 22 percent from other sources. In other words, the increase in oil consumption will be from 45 million bpd now to 80 million bpd in 1990. Most of the increase will have

TABLE 2

Estimated Crude Petroleum Reserves by Producing Country: 1975

Country	Proven Reserves of Oil (1,000 Barrels)	Percentage of World Proven Reserves
Arabian Peninsula, Iraq, Iran		
Saudi Arabia	148,600,000	22.5
Kuwait	68,000,000	10.3
Iran	64,500,000	9.7
Iraq	34,300,000	5.2
Neutral Zone	6,400,000	1.0
Abu Dhabi	29,500,000	4.4
Qatar	5,850,000	0.9
Oman	5,900,000	0.9
Dubai	1,350,000	0.2
Bahrain	312,000	0.05
Sharjah	1,350,000	0.2
Subtotal	366,062,000	55.35
Rest of Middle East		
Algeria	7,370,000	1.1
Egypt	3,900,000	0.6
Libya	26,100,000	4.0
Tunisia	1,065,000	0.2
Syria	2,240,000	0.3
Turkey	107,100	0.02
Subtotal	40,782,100	6.2
Other Major Producers		
Indonesia	14,000,000	2.1
United Kingdom	16,000,000	2.4
Norway	7,000,000	1.0
Nigeria	20,200,000	3.0
Venezuela	17,700,000	2.6

TABLE 2 (continued)

Estimated Crude Petroleum Reserves by Producing Country: 1975

Country	Proven Reserves of Oil (1,000 Barrels)	Percentage of World Proven Reserves
Other Major Producers (continued)		
United States	33,000,000	5.0
Soviet Union	80,400,000	12.2
People's Republic of China	20,000,000	3.0
Mexico	9,500,000	1.4
Canada	7,100,000	1.1
Total World	658,685,720	100.00

SOURCE: *Oil and Gas Journal*, December 1975.

to be supplied from resources in the Gulf region. The same report estimates that 15 years from now the United States will be importing 50 percent of its total petroleum needs, or about 12 million bpd.[40]

Access to most of this oil depends upon the ability of tankers to pass through the Straits of Hormuz and into the Gulf. In November 1971, Iran seized three tiny islands near the Straits— Abu Musa and Big and Little Tunb—all of which the Arabs regarded as their own. Iran, however, needed them for unquestionable control of the entrance to the Gulf. The country's military assistance to the Sultan of Oman is insurance against the possibility that a hostile power might gain control of the Arab shore of the Straits. Shah Muhammed Reza Pahlavi, in what might be called the Pahlavi Doctrine, has reserved for Iran the right to intervene directly against local regimes that might threaten the balance of power in the Gulf. In May 1973, before the drastic increases in petroleum prices, Arnaud de Borchgrave, a *Newsweek* correspondent, asked the Shah about Iran's military involvement against the Dhofar rebels in Oman: "Are you saying

[40]Report cited by Salah Muntasr, "Important Report Reveals the Struggle of the Arab Gulf," *Al-Ahram*, December 21, 1975.

you cannot tolerate radical regimes taking over any of the Arab sheikdoms?'' The Shah succintly replied, ''Yes.''[41] With the quintupling of oil prices since 1973, the Shah is all the more determined to apply his doctrine. Physical control of the Gulf gives Iran weight within OPEC equal to that of Saudi Arabia, whose strength in OPEC is due to its ability to affect world supply and price through the ease with which it can increase or restrict production.

Who can or could challenge the Shah's plan for regional hegemony? Iran is obviously no match for the Soviet Union, but since 1965–1966, indeed since the United States involvement in Vietnam and De Gaulle's break with NATO, Iran has increased economic exchanges with the Soviet Union and made itself more distant from United States foreign policy. It has purchased a limited amount of arms from the Soviet Union, contracted with the Soviets for a number of heavy industrial projects, and undertaken construction of a pipeline to deliver natural gas to southern Russia and Europe. It is speculated that Iran will soon ask for formal inclusion in the group of nations called the Non-Aligned.

These tentative steps to neutralize the regional influence of the Soviet Union should not obscure Iran's continued preference for the United States as its major supplier. Iran is still a member of CENTO and its purchases of military equipment from the United States have been spectacular: $4 billion in orders in 1973, $2 billion in 1974, and were approximately $4 billion for 1975–1976. Iran's total outlays for defense in the year 1975–76 were about $10 billion, despite cutbacks in other areas arising from decreased oil exports.[42] United States corporate investment in Iran

[41]Quoted in *Newsweek*, May 21, 1973, p. 44; similar views were presented in an interview with André Fontaine, *Le monde*, June 25, 1974.

[42]Marcel Barang, ''L'Iran, renaissance d'un empire,'' *Le monde diplomatique*, May 1975, p. 2. Another source, citing Defense Department figures, states that in fiscal year 1974, of a total of $8.3 billion in orders for military equipment, $3.8 billion came from Iran. Iran, along with Israel ($2.1 billion) and Saudi Arabia ($588 million), accounted for nearly 80 percent of United States military sales. Ali Banuazizi, ''Iran: The Making of a Regional Power,'' in A. L. Udovitch (ed.), *The Middle East: Oil, Conflict and Hope, Critical*

is substantial, and the American expatriate community there will soon reach 50,000. Finally, Iran must import more than 2 million tons of grain a year. Its only suppliers are Western, if not American. Iran's future, then, is very much bound up with the economic health of the noncommunist North. Through its control over the production of part of the energy supply needed by the North and its physical control over access to many non-Iranian oil fields, Iran can establish relations of mutual, rather than one-way, dependency.

Iran holds a military and economic edge over all its neighbors except the Soviet Union. The well-trained and well-equipped Turkish armed forces are formidable, but Turkey's primary military concerns are Cyprus, Greece, and the Soviet Union. Iran has offered Turkey financial assistance to help it meet its heavy payment problems resulting from increased oil prices. There are also joint projects afoot for improving the roads linking the two countries and for constructing an oil pipeline. Perhaps Iran can serve as a catalyst to the Regional Cooperation for Development (RCD), which since 1964 has drawn up plans for 54 projects, only 3 of which have been executed. Trade among the constituent states of the RCD has been less than $100 million per year.

Moreover, Iran need not fear a threat from Turkey because Turkish foreign policy is generally likely to remain preoccupied with NATO, the Balkans, and the EEC. Because of the Cyprus conflict and the imbroglio over continued United States arms supplies, Turkey's membership in NATO is being questioned in Ankara. At the same time, there has been a revival of interest in achieving cooperation among Balkan countries. Early in February 1976, representatives of Romania, Yugoslavia, Bulgaria, Greece, and Turkey met to discuss plans for regional cooperation. Balkan cooperation may become very important to Turkey as it begins to put distance between itself and the United States without overly exposing itself to the Soviet Union. In the mean-

---

Choices for Americans, vol. 10, Lexington Books, Lexington, Mass., 1976, pp. 463–506. The United States Congress has questioned Iran's ability to absorb this much sophisticated hardware, but after Secretary of State Kissinger's trip to Iran in August 1976, we were told to expect more of the same.

time, the economic future of Turkey depends largely on its dealings with the EEC. Turkish workers in EEC countries have been remitting annually over $1 billion in precious foreign exchange, but some of them have been laid off as a result of the recession in Europe. Since signing an accord in 1970, Turkey has begun a 22-year period of transition to full membership in the Common Market. In sum, Iran has little to fear from Turkey, whose attention is turned elsewhere but whose needs for petroleum and financing are such that enmity with Iran would have far-reaching consequences.

To the east, Pakistan—severed of Bangladesh—is militarily exposed to India. Iran, in effect, has extended its military umbrella over neutral Afghanistan and Pakistan; its activities include surveillance of the Baluchis, whose population lies on both sides of the Iran-Pakistan border. This role by no means entails Iranian hostility to India—at least so long as India and Pakistan do not go to war. Short of war, India will most likely continue to receive Iranian aid and supply iron ore for Iran's growing steel industry.

Iraq has been Iran's foremost regional adversary since the overthrow of Iraq's monarchy in 1958. Successive radical republican regimes gave asylum to Iranian political dissidents and used the Shi'ite religious centers of Nejaf and Kerbala to spread anti-Pahlavi propaganda among the Iranian population, although in Sunni-dominated Iraq the Shi'ite centers constitute a double-edged sword. The Iranians had a stronger card to play, however: their ability to support and protect the Kurdish insurrection in northern Iraq.

The Kurdish insurrection has had a strong impact upon Iraq's internal development during the last 15 to 30 years. While predominantly Sunni Muslims, the Kurds are ethnically and linguistically one of Iraq's myriad minorities. Most of the Kurds seek sanctuary—and indeed live—in Turkey and Iran, while a smaller group inhabits Syria. Iran provided sanctuary to the Kurdish tribes of Mulla Mustapha Barzani. Long, inconclusive clashes between the Iraqi army and the Kurds ended in March 1970 with an agreement between Barzani and the central authorities granting the Kurds some regional autonomy. The agree-

95

ment was never satisfactorily applied, and fighting broke out again. In the second round of fighting, Barzani appealed for aid from the United States, thereby confirming in the Arab mind many of the charges that he was serving Iranian, Israeli, and United States interests. The fighting between 1974 and 1975 was particularly intense. While some supplies and arms reached Barzani through Iran, the Soviet-equipped Iraqi army and air force launched an all-out assault against Barzani's mountain strongholds. One would logically suspect that Kuwait, Syria, Iran, and Israel found nothing inconvenient in this allocation of Iraqi military priorities. Nonetheless, in March 1975 the Shah, resorting to the mediation of Boumedienne, arrived at an entente with Iraqi Vice President Saddam Hussein, whereby Iran would deny sanctuaries to Barzani's Pesh Mirga fighters and in exchange Iraq would grant a general amnesty for all those Kurds who wished to lay down their arms and rejoin Iraq. A modus vivendi for the use of the Shatt al-Arab was also part of the agreement. The point here, however, is not so much the details of the agreement, but rather that Iran conclusively demonstrated to Iraq that it held the key to a seemingly interminable struggle. For the moment, the Iranians saw no further interest in keeping alive the struggle of the Kurds led by Barzani—perhaps because they feared the rebellion would spread to other Kurds living in Iran—but it is highly possible that the Kurdish movement could be reactivated. In 1976–1977 new pockets of armed Kurdish resistance were widely reported, but if there was outside assistance involved it came from Syria, not Iran. To assure that the Kurds remain under control will require considerable circumspection on the part of the Iraqis in their dealings with Iran.

For Baghdad, settling the Kurdish rebellion was and is a question of life or death, for the Kurdish areas include Iraq's major oil fields. During the 15 years that the Kurds and the central authorities oscillated between compromise and war, the economy suffered immensely and the army had its hands constantly full. One wonders how lasting the current entente can be, given the ambitions of both countries. Some incident, such as the dispute over the Spanish Sahara that now divides Algeria and Morocco, could easily upset this tactical accord. The equally tactical accord that the Shah has made with Hafez al-Assad of Syria further diminishes Iraq's room for maneuver.[43]

Saudi Arabia is the only remaining neighbor with pretensions to military and political weight in the Gulf, but in this case, too, Iran has successfully outmaneuvered its Wahhabi rival. The Shah has dropped all Iranian claims to Bahrain, thus toning down the image of Iranian expansionism. Most of the Emirates see the more immediate threat to their territorial integrity as Saudi Arabia or Iraq, and all concerned implicitly understand that Iran is prepared to intervene to protect any of the sheikdoms. The Shah has also passed over the heads of the Saudis and dealt directly with Cairo. In May 1974, before either Saudi Arabia or Kuwait had made much of an effort to help Egypt with its non-military financial needs, Iran worked out a $1 billion package in loans, commodity purchase credits, project credits, and grants. The Shah thereby ostentatiously demonstrated his one-upman-ship over Egypt's Arab brethren. King Faisal of Saudi Arabia hurriedly offered Egypt assistance, but Iran had shown Egypt and Saudi Arabia that Cairo need not rely solely upon one patron.

The emerging Pax Iranica is founded upon the structural and circumstantial weaknesses of all its regional neighbors. Iranian hegemony will depend on the maintenance of these weaknesses. Like Saudi Arabia, Iran has an interest in the status quo, but over the long term Iran may be the more insistent of the two nations in perpetuating divisions among the other states of the region. Saudi Arabia and Iran are both crucial to United States geopolitical interests, and in most instances (except the nonset-tlement of the Arab-Israeli dispute) Tehran and Riyadh act with Washington's blessing.

[43]Assad's state visit to Tehran took place at the end of December 1975. Relations that had been broken since 1966 were not restored at the ambas-sadorial level until June 1974. Iran has come out since 1973 with more pro-Arab pronouncements than in the past, although it still maintains relations with Israel. Iran has loaned Syria $80 million and promised another $70 million. Iran may also help Syria finance petroleum imports, since the supply from Iraq is now in question. Simultaneously, Iraq and Turkey are negotiating for a pipeline by which the Iraqis could deliver up to 25 million tons of petroleum per year to Turkey, perhaps at a discount.

The Palestinians

The Palestinians are a diaspora, not a region. In assessing their role in the area, the important point to keep in mind is that the camp dwellers and guerrillas are only one among several Palestinian constituencies that have diverse, occasionally contradictory, interests. All share a common sense of injustice, their demand for the recognition of their right to reclaim territory, and their conviction of having been mistreated by just about everybody—not only by the Zionists, but by the Arabs and the great powers as well. In the broadest sense, then, the Palestinians are the spoilers, a group that feels that nothing it can lose is as valuable as what it could or should gain.

Most Arab regions, and certainly the front-line states, are painfully inching their way toward a tactical accommodation with Israel. But what the Israelis regard as too little in the way of concessions, most Palestinians regard as far too much. Thus, when groups such as Black September and others resort to international terrorism or kidnapping to expose the Arab accommodationists, most Palestinians probably draw some satisfaction from the spectacles. Still, it is too easy to assume that the diaspora is preoccupied only by violence and intransigence.

There are several distinct Palestinian communities, each of which differs in life-style and source of livelihood.[44] First, an international community of intellectuals and technocrats are primarily scattered throughout the Gulf states and the Arabian peninsula but are also prominent in Lebanon and North America. They live comfortably and have earned social status and professional respect, yet it is they who must articulate the Palestinian cause abroad. Some have abandoned their careers to join the

[44]See Abd al-Moneim al-Mashatt, "The Distribution of the Palestinian People Outside Palestine," *International Politics* (Egypt), no. 42, October 1975, pp. 57–64; and Nabil Shaath, "Palestinian High-Level Manpower," *Journal of Palestine Studies*, vol. 1, no. 2, Winter 1972, pp. 80–95. For a sensitive account of the 150,000 to 200,000 Palestinians in Kuwait, see Trudy Rubin, "What Do the Palestinians Want?: The Palestinians in Kuwait," *Alicia Patterson Foundation Newsletter*, New York, June 1975.

guerrillas, and most give financial support to the resistance, but the extent of their intransigence is moot. Another group, most prominent in Lebanon and the West Bank and Gaza, are the camp dwellers. While the camp dwellers have relatively little to lose, before the civil war in Lebanon al-Fatah was as preoccupied with bettering their working conditions as with launching raids into northern Israel. Access to jobs plays an equally important role for the Palestinians of the West Bank and Gaza. A third community consists of the Palestinians of Israel, who have been cut off from the other communities since 1948. Finally, there are the guerrilla movements themselves, which dominate the headlines through terrorist activities.

In short, when it is said that the Palestinians are part of the rejection front, it must be remembered that there are various levels of rejection (or willingness to compromise) sustained by different economic and social expectations. Yet, as a group, the Palestinians keep the attention of the Arab world focused on the confrontation with Israel. The symbols and substance of this confrontation are national identity and territory, that is, the essence of nineteenth-century romantic nationalism. Inasmuch as the Arabs see the North as Israel's sponsor, the terms of debate and the popular perception of what is at issue are cast in a form that misses the essence of the economic stake between rich and poor. Still, among the most militantly leftist Palestinians, a clear conceptual and ideological link has been made between the territorial displacement of their people and the economic dependency of the South upon the North. The kidnapping of the OPEC oil ministers at Vienna in December 1975 by "Carlos" and his colleagues was a theatrical enactment of the linkage. When the hostages were separated into three groups—friends, neutrals, and enemies—the Saudi and Iranian ministers were put in the enemy group; the rest, including Kuwaitis, were not. OPEC, the most successful of all Third World bargaining agencies, was put on notice of the necessity to tie economic gains to political causes. The singling out of Saudi Arabia and Iran in this dramatic fashion emphasized that the radicals regarded those states as the major agents of cosmetic reform and of accommodation with the United States at the expense of the Palestinians.

SUMMARY

From the lengthy presentation of relations among states in the various subregions of the Middle East, the following conclusions, having direct bearing upon Middle Eastern development and North-South relations, may be drawn.

1. The Middle East has, roughly, four "worlds" of its own. The first is composed of the oil-rich states having sophisticated economies. They will be the poles of regional integration if it ever occurs. The second is made up of oil-rich, surplus-earning states, which, with the exception of Libya, serve as brokers between the interests of the North and the Third and Fourth Worlds of the Middle East. The Third World consists of the oil-less but relatively advanced economies of the region, while the Fourth World is made up of the poor, primarily rural states on the Arab periphery. They all compete among themselves for access to what the North has to offer, or for access to the clients of the North in the region.

2. Economic and political integration among states and subregions is minimal or nonexistent.

3. The exclusive frame of reference for policy making and economic planning is the nation-state.

4. With a few exceptions, each state feels that with the proper mix of policies and luck it can achieve its own economic and political sovereignty.

5. The pursuit of national interest may undermine, intentionally or unintentionally, the national interests of other regional neighbors. This is particularly true in the interstate competition for foreign exchange, technology, and arms—or precisely the goods the North controls.

6. Bilateralism prevails over multilateralism, and individualistic bargaining prevails over collective approaches.

7. The Arab-Israeli conflict sustains a preoccupation with questions of political sovereignty and territorial rights even as the North-South dialogue is centered on issues of the global redistribution of wealth.

THREE

The Middle East in
North-South Relations

The socioeconomic stratification of the Middle East and the tendency of the states in the region to pursue independent paths of development based on perceptions of *national* self-interest lead to various—and often conflicting—attitudes toward negotiations with Northern industrial states. These differing attitudes, in turn, impede the adoption of collective bargaining strategies in North-South negotiating forums. To the extent that opinions and analyses of North-South relations are articulated in the Middle East, they present a spectrum of approaches and conclusions reflected in the following quotations.

Finally, it is necessary to take into account the fact that imperialism is a world system, the highest stage of capitalism, and that it must be defeated in world-wide confrontation. The strategic purpose of this struggle must be the destruction of imperialism.[45]

Che Guevara

Even if the final goal is the liquidation of the world capitalist order, struggle toward this revolutionary goal must not overlook any short- and medium-term reformist measures that could raise the standard of living of the masses of the Third World.[46]

Ismail Sabry Abdullah, Director of
Institute of National Planning, Egypt

[45]Guevara was addressing the Organization for the Solidarity of the Peoples of Africa, Asia, and Latin America, April 16, 1967. Cited by Pierre Jalée, *The Third World in World Economy*, Monthly Review Press, New York, 1969, p. 141.

[46]From Ismail Sabry Abdullah, "The New World Economic Order: The Urgent Issues at Dispute," *Al-Tali'a*, vol. 12, no. 2, February 1976, p. 68, in Arabic.

Q. Between ourselves, Yamani, is it really in your interest to push us over the brink?

A. In Saudi Arabia we don't think so. We know if your economy collapses, we'll collapse with you. . . . In other words, unless the countries of the West are prosperous, we can't import your industry and your technology. We're not at all interested in seeing you collapse, neither for political reasons, since we're fighting communism, nor for economic ones. I'll go further; I don't believe the other OPEC countries are either, be they pro-Western like Kuwait, Abu Dhabi, or Iran, pro-Eastern like Iraq, or neutral like Algeria. But there's a problem: not all of them believe that a new increase in oil prices will lead to disaster.[47]

Sheikh Ahmed Zaki Yamani

THE DOMESTIC SALIENCE OF THE NORTH-SOUTH DIALOGUE

These variegated attitudes are only fitting given the disparities that characterize the region. Yet differing opinions, like the contexts from which they emerge, are upon closer scrutiny interwoven with elements of sameness. The many ideological stances and analytic approaches are the products of national intellectual and technocratic elites who share a fairly common degree of contact with the outside world, a high level of educational attainment, and high standards of living. But, for the masses, questions of the world economic order—in striking contrast, for example, with the threat of direct imperial control or the presence of Israel—have little or no emotive impact. The Western automobile driver or home-heater may be far more sensitive to some of the issues involved in the call for a new international economic order than one of the mass of Middle Easterners. The debate thus takes place in a rarefied atmosphere, with the radicals and conservatives eating at the same table.

The elites are intermediaries between the rich North and the poor South. On the one hand, their education, standard of living, and life-style set them apart from their own peoples (a fact of which most are acutely aware); on the other hand, their ideology,

[47]Fallaci, ''A Sheik Who Hates to Gamble.''

ethics, or patriotism set them apart from persons in advanced consumerist societies whose habits they variously share. At once adversaries and brokers of the prevailing order, Middle Eastern elites are in the throes of establishing the consistency of their own roles.

The upshot in terms of North-South bargaining is this: Northern elites bargain in the name of the middle- and lower-middle-class majorities of their societies whose consumption is stimulated by and sustains the corporate industrial interests that are the backbone of Northern economies. Northern elites are an extension of the middle-class majority of their societies. Southern elites, in contrast, are not really an extension of Southern populations but another beast altogether. Southern middle classes, to begin with, are a distinct minority among the mass of illiterate or quasi-educated peasants or urban workers. In addition, Southern demands and bargaining strategy, by their very nature, must be formulated and articulated by the technocratic and managerial elites who grew up as part of a vulnerable, culturally distinct, upper-middle-class minority. In other words, many of the advocates of global justice are in the very awkward position of being members of a privileged class within their own societies.

Some Middle Eastern societies are more egalitarian than others, but all manifest a sharp economic cleavage between the top 5 percent of the population and the bottom 50 or 60 percent. A 1969 government survey of household budgets in Iran revealed one of the sharpest skews in the Middle East: The lowest fifth of households accounted for only 4 percent of all consumption expenditure, while the top fifth accounted for 56 percent.[48] While the skew of Iranian income distribution is particularly pronounced, the marked gaps common to all societies of the region remorselessly cut across political and ideological cleavages. The elites in question enjoy not only a standard of living but a style of life that is identifiably Northern (or Western): cars, villas,

[48]Banuazizi, "Iran: The Making of a Regional Power," p. 482. Note also that in Egypt there has been confiscatory taxation since 1961 on all gross incomes exceeding £E 10,000 (or about $20,000). Still, an income after taxes of £E 7,000 is 70 times the average per capita income. New legislation will ease the tax burden on higher incomes and the ratio may go to 200 to 1.

telephones, television, suits and ties, summer vacations, record collections, whiskey, and birthday parties for their children. No more, in short, than the norms of suburbia, but in the Third World the pattern constitutes an economic and cultural world apart—one which, moreover, the elites would not willingly abandon. Yet the elites espouse development because the plight of the masses is so obvious, and because in the absence of development the elites themselves would become further isolated from the masses and thus vulnerable to their wrath.

The Southern—or at any rate, the Middle Eastern—elites are only too well aware that those who bargain for the North are more representative of their own societies than those who bargain for the South. It is therefore difficult for these Southern elites to make their demands, threats, and bluffs credible. When Yamani or any other Arab leader threatens to keep the oil in the ground and go back to the tent for the rest of his days, who is to take him seriously? Libya's Colonel Qaddafi might go through with such a threat, but doing so would probably lead the rest of the Libyan Revolutionary Command Council to abandon him to his fate.

Along the same lines, it is important to stress that the small groups actively involved in North-South bargaining are a minority within a minority. The major issues stemming from the demands for a new world economic order are fundamentally economic and technological in nature. Commodity pricing, debt management, indexing, preferential trade relations, buffer stocks, technology transfers, and so on down a long list are subjects that are best dealt with by specialists rather than by heads of state (with the possible exception of the Shah, who is reputedly an expert in energy matters) or other generalists. The four commissions that began to meet in Paris after February 11, 1976, within the framework of the Conference on International Economic Cooperation (CIEC) reflect this fact. The experts, of necessity, have gained their expertise in the North or, at least, in Northern institutions in the region, such as the American University in Beirut. Petroleum engineers, economic planners, mathematical modelers, nuclear physicists, market analysts, geologists, business managers, and the like are the backbone of the negotiating teams. Especially important among them are those experts who have served in the International Bank for Reconstruction and Development (IBRD), the IMF, such specialized agencies of the United Nations as its Conference on Trade and Development (UNCTAD), and the regional equivalents of these bodies such as the Arab League's special agencies, the administrators of local development funds, or the CAEU. Work in these international bodies has given Middle Eastern technocrats professional status and a high standard of living, putting them on a par in both respects with their Northern colleagues. And the new wealth generally available in the Middle East has brought back to the region technocrats who had gone to the North to build their careers.

All this is quite obvious but easily forgotten. These Middle Eastern elites stand in relation to their societies much as the North stands collectively in relation to the South. They sense instinctively the potential violence that lies in the poverty of their own countries, which could lead to the destruction of their own favored positions.[49] It is, analogously, perceptions of the long-term consequences of Southern poverty that have moved the North to consider some compromise on redistribution of wealth and resources.

Middle Eastern elites thus need the cooperation of the North in order to maintain their own positions. The nature of this dependency varies from country to country. In Iran, Saudi Arabia, Lebanon, Tunisia, and Morocco, the umbilical cord between local business and technocratic elites and Northern multinational corporations is openly exposed. Egypt is a more complex case. In 1961, Nasser launched what was called a socialist revolution, but one that was never intended to bleed the middle classes for the sake of the poor. The standard of living of the poor was to be raised by placing medium and heavy industry, banking, and foreign trade under state control. All surpluses from these sec-

[49]This observation is hardly new. See inter alia, Samir Amin, *Le développement inégal*, Éditions de minuit, Paris, 1973, p. 186; and Richard Fagen, "Equity in the South in the Context of North-South Relations," in *Rich and Poor Nations in the World Economy*, McGraw-Hill for the Council on Foreign Relations, New York, 1978.

tors were then to be pumped back into new investments and expanded social services. But for a number of reasons the surpluses never materialized, the public sector failed to generate foreign exchange through exports, and Egypt, already a food-deficit country, became dependent upon outside sources of foreign exchange and food aid. For Nasser's middle-class regime, the parting of the ways came between 1965 and 1967. The response to Egypt's economic problems could have been either intensification of the socialist revolution through stringent measures to limit middle-class consumption and mobilize domestic savings or greater reliance on foreign borrowing and deficit financing. Nasser never conclusively chose one course or the other. His successor, Anwar el-Sadat, chose the second course. Egypt's open-door policy will reinforce middle-class consumerism and the dependence of technocratic, managerial, and business elites on Western enterprises and sources of capital. Whether these enter Egypt directly or through intermediaries such as Saudi Arabia, Iran, and Kuwait makes little difference. Much the same sort of economic and class evolution seems to be taking place in the Sudan.

Iraq, Syria, and Algeria are somewhat different cases. The ideal of socialist equality seems to have penetrated more deeply into the consciences of elites and masses in these countries than in Egypt. The regimes manifest a somewhat greater degree of austerity, of living close to the people, than do others. But all this is a matter of degree, not of kind. Many elite members in all three countries are getting rich; payoffs, kickbacks, shakedowns, and the like are not uncommon; and state business with Northern partners is increasing rapidly. Can these elites do business with the multinational corporations for any extended length of time without being on the take?[50]

In their role as bargaining agents in North-South encounters, however, Middle Eastern elites have one gaping hole in their

[50]Increasingly one hears that corruption and ostentatious spending are becoming the norms in Algeria (witness the widespread allegations of this during the debates on the new National Charter in 1976) and in Syria. See Eric Rouleau, "La Syrie dans le bourbier libanais," *Le monde*, in five parts, June 1–5, 1976, especially Part 4, "Le pourrissement."

armor: their unwillingness to put their own Northern way of life on the line in the name of Southern demands. It seems fair to presume that the North will not make concessions to the South purely out of a sense of humanity or a concern with equity. Concessions will come as a result of real or implied, but above all, credible threats. Trade wars, embargoes, decoupling, and even political and armed combat are all plausible threats. Yet every one of them would entail material sacrifices for the middle classes, the disruption of careers, and—were new and more radical regimes to emerge in the heat of confrontation—the overthrow of the elites themselves. For all these reasons current elites, whatever their ideological divergencies, tend to seek accommodation in their negotiations with the North.

Although Middle Eastern public opinion is not yet involved in the issues that make up the North-South debate, it would not take much to draw the masses in. The reason is simple. Unlike the Western automobile driver, the Middle Eastern masses know the issues in rudimentary form; what they do not know is their contemporary packaging. Any Egyptian who has been exposed to the bare bones of his nation's recent history will know of the unequal exchange between Egypt's cotton fields and the mills of Lancashire and Manchester; so, too, any Algerian can grasp the relations between France's wine industry and the vineyards of Oranie. Whatever its religious and cultural overtones, imperialism in the Middle East took the form of political control for economic advantage, and the conceptual linkage of politics and economics has never subsequently been lost upon the area's masses.

During the epoch of direct imperial control and colonization, Middle Eastern bourgeois elites, regardless of left-right cleavages, were at one in their recognition of the economic underpinnings of European control as well as in their quest for national political sovereignty. In a general sense, they believed that if a country could affirm its political sovereignty it could then master its economic fate. In the wake of World War II, however, this notion was rapidly dispelled, as most Middle Eastern nations achieved formal independence. In the process, ideological cleavages among dominant elites became acute. Political sovereignty proved to mean relatively little, while military alliances, capital flows, currency blocs, and the terms of trade came to the fore. But mass opinion could not focus upon these problems, whose anonymity and complexity defy even the most sophisticated audiences. The debate about neoimperialism seldom spilled over into the public arena except—and they are major exceptions— in the directly felt presence of Israel or in major North-South encounters such as the Algerian war of independence.

After political sovereignty was formally achieved by most states in the Middle East, the cudgels of anti-neoimperialist ideology were wielded largely by the Marxist and neo-Marxist left. Many non-Marxist figures, including all heads of state in the Middle East in the 1950s and 1960s, lashed out at the forces of neoimperialism. But after Prime Minister Muhammed Mossadegh nationalized the Iranaian oil industry in 1953, the vocabulary and the structure of the attack were distinctly leftist.[51] The Algerian war for independence until 1962, the United States–Cuban confrontation, the protracted war in Vietnam during the 1960s, and the emergence of the Palestinian guerrillas after 1967 affirmed the symbols of violent confrontation with the world capitalist order so compellingly articulated by Franz Fanon and, of course, by Che Guevara.

But the nationalist elites of the Middle East found themselves ambivalent as far as their attitudes toward the use of violence or even direct confrontation were concerned. Although many judged necessary a major adjustment of the terms of trade between rich and poor, they hoped that adjustment could be achieved without resort to head-on collisions and perhaps out of the enlightened self-interest of the rich. Moreover, in the 1960s, Soviet aid and assistance provided support for national development that the nonsocialist West had failed to do. By the end of the decade, however, the impression had grown that the socialist countries exacted terms of exchange as hard as the West's, and for inferior goods. The dilemma remained: How could

---

[51]See, for example, Egypt's National Charter of May 1962, the Algerian Tripoli Program of the same year, and the 1964 Charter of Algiers.

each Middle Eastern country achieve national prosperity and a real welfare state while safeguarding political and economic sovereignty? The 1960s provided no answers to this question short of war between the rich and the poor.

The way out that was pursued subsequently (and it may well be one if not the only possible solution to the dilemma) was to devise a strategy to bargain for a new world economic order. The issue remained global inequality or inequity, but it bears repeating that in its contemporary form it is the conscious concern of very few. This is hardly surprising, since the concept of a new world economic order requires a conceptual abandonment of national frames of reference, an intellectual step of great difficulty for elites whose major preoccupation has been affirming national sovereignty. Further, international economic issues have generally been subsumed by the overriding concern with confrontation with Israel. Thus, while it is undeniable that the oil embargo and price increase of 1973 were the catalysts both for a growing sense of urgency among industrialized nations regarding the need to reach accommodation with primary producers and for the producers' awareness of their potential power, these actions were considered in the region itself (Turkey and Iran excepted) primarily as effective tools for eroding the special relationship between Israel and the United States. In other words, the policy makers of the Middle East accurately perceived the economic power at their disposal, but pegged its use—this time with the exception of the Algerians—to leverage in an ossified geopolitical dispute. In sum, it can be said that there has been far more sophisticated analysis of the issues at hand in the industrialized nations and Latin America than in the Middle East. Those segments of local technocracies that have participated in the debate have been drawn in through their contacts with, say, UNCTAD and the UN Industrial Development Organization (UNIDO), the Group of 77, the Third World Forum of Mexico, the Bariloche Institute of Argentina, or Jan Tinbergen's task force under the auspices of the Club of Rome. Outside their limited ranks, awareness of issues is very low. Local magazines do not run cover stories, as have *Time* and *Newsweek*, on the looming struggle between North and South. At the same time, the sheer quantity of international meetings and the subsequent, albeit perfunctory, local newspaper coverage of their proceedings will surely alter this situation in the near future.

Perceptions of the need for a new global deal are currently widely enough shared among Southern elites so that they have allowed the non-Marxist bourgeoisie to rejoin the process of analyzing and devising strategies to combat neoimperialism. In so doing, the non-Marxists have assimilated some of the vocabulary, if not the convictions, of the Marxists and neo-Marxists. In the Middle East, the two most vocal proponents of a new order are President Boumedienne of Algeria and the Shah of Iran. Neither, of course, is a Marxist. While Boumedienne does stand considerably to the left of the Shah, the courses of action both men espouse in confronting the North are, on the whole, similar. Both men believe that the new order need not arise from the ashes of the old; that if confrontation proves necessary, it should be used for tactical purposes to promote accommodation; and that the health of Northern economies is vital to that of Southern economies.

This view, with a few minor exceptions, is common to the elites of the area. It is in a way an act of faith, perhaps misplaced, in the inexhaustible capacity of the old order to generate its own transformation. It is an act of faith that Northern technology and self-interest will create new sources of wealth and, in cooperation with the South, provide for their redistribution. It is an accommodationist, variable-sum image of the future, bullish when the North has become increasingly bearish. In the post-armed-revolutionary phase, then, national bourgeoisies, regardless of left-right cleavages, are united in their goal of a new order. This was the case, as we have noted, at an earlier period when the goal was national political sovereignty. The major difference is that the present goal cannot be precisely defined either in time or in scope. But that imprecision may be more of an asset to these elites than a liability.

MIDDLE EAST BARGAINING WITH THE NORTH:
INSTRUMENTS AND THEMES

Those who in the past had no voice in world affairs now realize that they are the majority of humanity and that they possess resources essential to the continued prosperity of the West. They have become cognizant of their strength, not merely their rights.[52]

Ismail Sabry Abdullah

[T]wo thirds of all petroleum produced moves in international trade. . . . For this reason the position of the petroleum exporters is unique; it is hard to conceive of any combination of producer cartels that would have as much effect on world trade in the next few years as an increase of even one dollar in the price of oil.[53]

Hollis B. Chenery

We say to world capitalism that its methods of dealing with us are rejected and we shall combat them. But at the outset, we must offer an alternative and it lies in a reasonable solution to the problem of all raw and strategic materials without exception. To achieve this just solution necessitates that we exercise complete national control over our resources. The question here is not one of socialism but rather of national sovereignty, of life and death as regards us all, we, the children of the Third World.[54]

Houari Boumedienne

In what follows we shall look more closely at the organizational and thematic approaches various Middle Eastern constituencies have adopted in bargaining with the North and, derivatively, with one another. Without the war of October 1973 and the ensuing oil price-hikes, it is conceivable that the crystallization of the major issues in the dialogue would have proceeded no more quickly than in the preceding decade. But because of the events of 1973, the issues became unavoidable and critical. Con-

[52]Ismail Sabry Abdullah, "The New World Economic Order and the Struggle for Economic Liberation," *Al-Tali'a*, vol. 11, no. 11, November 1975, p. 17.

[53]Hollis B. Chenery, "Restructuring the World Economy," *Foreign Affairs*, vol. 53, no. 2, January 1975, p. 245.

[54]Lutfi al-Kholi, *In the Revolution, about the Revolution, by the Revolution: Conversations with Boumedienne*, Dar al-Qadaya, Beirut, 1975, p. 200. Boumedienne voiced similar views as early as 1965 (see p. 128).

sidering the extent to which the Middle East, more than any other region, has sensitized the world to the crisis of global redistribution, the lack of awareness of most Middle Eastern elites about what they have set in motion is surprising.

There are a number of instruments and forums through which Middle Eastern policy makers can become familiar with the principal issues of the new world economic order and establish bargaining positions vis-à-vis the North. The most effective of these instruments has been OPEC, the foremost raw materials cartel in the world. But only oil exporters can join OPEC, much less play a role within it. Moreover, OPEC has seldom couched its demands in the wider terms of North-South confrontation. So while OPEC is the "hardest" of the instrumentalities under consideration, it is also the most exclusive in membership and the narrowest in focus.

A second set of instruments comprises those forums through which direct negotiations with the North may take place and which can be used by most states in the Middle East: UNCTAD, the CIEC, the IMF, the IBRD, UNIDO, and the Euro-Arab Dialogue. None of these forums has been singled out by Middle Eastern policymakers as a venue for North-South encounters, mainly for two reasons: First, North-South issues are not sufficiently pressing that policymakers are actually searching for such an arena; second, to date none of these forums have produced results favorable to Middle Eastern or other Southern states.

Bilateral negotiations between Middle Eastern states and a Northern government or business are yet a third instrumentality for bargaining. Arranging supplies credits, commodity loans, and project loans with individual Northern states is a process that seldom stops. In addition, Egypt, among others, has bargained with the EEC for grain supplies on favorable terms, while several Middle Eastern countries have repeatedly gone to bank consortiums in the North for Eurodollar loans. Because of the emphasis on the initiative of individual states rather than on collective approaches, many of the transactions with the North fall under this rubric.

There are also several forums more or less limited to Southern members in which bargaining positions can be debated and clarified. For Middle Eastern states, these consist primarily of the Group of 77, the Non-Aligned, the Arab League, and the OAU. Seldom have any of these forums issued specific policy declarations that have had any binding effect upon participating states. For instance, the members of OPEC attending the Colombo meeting of the Non-Aligned in the summer of 1976 refused to endorse a resolution to proclaim an embargo on oil shipments to France, which persists in selling arms to South Africa. Nonetheless, these bodies do serve to sensitize the participants to each other's concerns, thus enabling them to gauge the intensity with which certain causes are espoused and therefore to judge where compromises might be struck. They permit the exchange of diplomatic favors and the floating of "policy balloons." They will not, however, be the cutting edge of North-South encounters.

Finally, there are analytic and intellectual forums at which problems are defined and long-range scenarios worked out in a scholarly manner. These consist of "think tanks" and international bodies of experts managed and brought together by entities such as the Tinbergen Group, the Bariloche Institute, the Third World Forum, and the CAEU. It is within these forums that the issues in the North-South confrontation have been most carefully defined. Similarly, in preparation for the most recent meeting of UNCTAD (Nairobi, 1976), regional planning institutes around the globe were called upon to work up background studies and careful briefing papers for the conferees.

What sort of issues have been dealt with in this manner? A perhaps typical delineation of priorities was presented by Alphonse Aziz and Mabid al-Jarhi of Egypt's Institute of National Planning in advance of UNCTAD IV. The following are the issues they analyzed and the policies they advocated:

1. A nonreciprocal tariff reduction on Third World industrial exports to the North of no less than 10 percent.

2. A five-year moratorium on debt payments along with the waiving of interest charges during the same period.

3. Reduction of interest rates on all loans to Third World countries to 2.5 percent or less.

4. An increase in financial transfer from the developed to the developing countries of 10 percent by 1976 (or presumably 1977).

5. Establishment of a system whereby OECD countries would match OPEC's level of foreign aid and socialist countries would attain 30 percent of OPEC's level.

6. A debt fund that would lend to developing countries according to their per capita GNP. Under this arrangement, countries whose per capita income was less than $250 would receive 70 percent of the fund's loans. The fund would be financed by a 0.01 percent levy on f.o.b. value of exports of all countries.

7. Establishment of a new lending fund to the Third World.[55]

Different states attach different priorities to these and other proposed reforms. This limits the possibility of devising a common strategy. For instance, Egypt is particularly concerned by growing indebtedness to the North, which by 1975 had reached $120 billion for all the Third World. Servicing on this debt reached an annual rate equivalent to 50 percent of all development aid extended to the South by the North. Egypt's foreign debt, exclusive of short-term credits but including military obligations, is on the order of $15 billion; its debt-servicing payments have run as high as 40 percent of export earnings.[56] Although Egypt's external debt is its most pressing economic problem, it has not solicited the aid of other nations in the same plight in trying to solve it. There has been no discernible effort, for instance, to put together a common front with the other most heavily indebted

[55] Alphonse Aziz and Mabid al-Jarhi, "Aggravation of External Equilibrium of the LDCs and the New International Economic Order," in Aziz and Jarhi, *The New International Economic Order and UNCTAD IV*, pp. 11–12.

[56] It is particularly difficult to ascertain actual ratios precisely because the total military debt figure has not been officially made public, and servicing the debt to the Soviet Union is partially scheduled within annually negotiated frame agreements between the two countries. For Egypt's position on Third World debt, see Ahmad Izzedin Hilal (Minister of Petroleum), address to the Seventh Special Session of the United Nations General Assembly, September 1975, in *Petroleum* (Cairo), vol. 12, no. 3, September–October 1975, pp. 10–14.

states in the area (the Sudan, Jordan, Tunisia, the Yemens, Somalia, and Syria).

Industrialization and technology transfer are of vital concern to nearly all Middle Eastern states. Once again differing foreign exchange positions lead to differing strategies and, in most instances, to bilateral approaches. The only exceptions to this rule are the CAEU and the Center for Arab Industrialization, which are striving to achieve a rational distribution of industry within the Arab world by relying on multinational Arab companies and multilateral financing.[57] So far, these bodies have simply designated sectors of obvious interest: refining, petrochemicals and fertilizers, mining, and processing, cement, steel, and pharmaceuticals.

Neither of these bodies nor any group of states have worked out a common policy on the terms of industrial and technological transfer. Further, the whole question of how to deal with and police the multinational corporations has scarcely been broached. Among the issues that appear to have received little attention, for example, are the likely behavior of established chemical giants as opposed to that of new chemical firms, the parceling out of regional and extraregional markets, the setting of common policies on tariff protection, and the structuring of equity positions in joint ventures. A few general platitudes inform national policymakers: (1) the Middle East has capital resources and local markets to attract Northern industry; (2) the trend is to move industry closer to the source of its raw material inputs; (3) the Middle East is geographically suited to supply new Northern markets in Asia and Africa. Beyond these simple assumptions, the ostensible policy is to let the chips fall where they may. In the petrochemical sector they may fall on the major oil companies intent on pursuing their two-decade-old efforts to encroach upon the products and markets of the established chemical firms. In trying to improve their market shares, the

[57]See, for example, Kemal Maqsud, "The New International Economic Order and the Industrialization of the Arab Countries" in Aziz and Jarhi, *The New International Economic Order and UNCTAD IV*. In general, all Arab pronouncements are in favor of the resolution taken at the Lima meeting of UNIDO (March 12–16, 1975) calling for an increase in the Third World's share of manufacturing from 7 percent in 1975 to 25 percent by the year 2000.

outsiders . . . will have few qualms about subsequently exporting to world markets and "disrupting" the positions of "majors"; secondly, MNE's [multinational enterprises] will be "integrating" world markets. Their interest in promoting, say, inter-Arab exports in the manner some exponents of regional integration have desired will be secondary or nonexistent, and, to the extent one MNE appears to be gaining an advantage in one country in the region, other oligopolists may be tempted to match it in other countries. Such behavior will not facilitate regional political integration through joint planning and facilities allocation. Countries of the region may also end up competing with one another in giving favorable energy costs and financing to ventures involving MNEs.[58]

However valid these apprehensions may be, they have been shunted aside in the rush for the acquisition of technology.

Middle East countries with sound foreign exchange positions have the luxury of choosing the technology and the partner they want. They are not under immediate pressure to bargain collectively over the pricing and financing of the transfer. The others, like Egypt, have to worry about the terms of transfer but are too foreign-exchange-poor to bargain effectively. Nor can they choose their partners. They are strapped into frame agreements with the socialist and some Third World countries or into bilateral credit agreements whereby they must import the technology of the creditor. Egypt might be eager to pursue Sabry Abdullah's call for a world market for technological know-how. (Sabry Abdullah contends that the current costs of technological know-how have been determined in a quasi-monopolistic manner.)[59] But, again, no collective position has emerged because the oil-rich do not yet have to worry about such costs.

A potential conflict lies in the debate over capital- versus labor-intensive industries. Egypt, for instance, has no official policy

[58]Lawrence G. Franko, "Prospects for Industrial Joint Ventures in the Oil Exporting Countries of the Middle East and North Africa," OECD Development Center, Paris, August 1975, p. 13.

[59]Sabry Abdullah, "The New World Economic Order and the Struggle for Economic Liberation," p. 79. Franko, "Industrial Joint Ventures," rightly points out that labor-intensive processes require a very high level of managerial skills.

on this question. Yet planners such as Sabry Abdullah have warned that the tendency to import the most advanced kinds of industrial technology may simply condemn traditional modes of production rather than try to reform them. He cites the textile industry as a particularly acute case of this phenomenon. Moreover, he argues that the capital-intensive, advanced technology approach snuffs out the innovative spirit of local manufacturers while reinforcing dependency upon the handful of states that export technology.[60] The Algerians, however, are convinced that only the most advanced industrial processes will permit Third World countries to export their manufactures on a competitive basis. For countries like Saudi Arabia, labor, not capital, is the limiting factor.

A final issue that has been minimally aired in the Middle East is that of the exportation of "dirty" industries from the North to the South, placing the burden of industrial pollution and disposal of waste on the shoulders of Third World economies. Egypt, one feels, would be only too happy to accept this burden, as would, perhaps, most other states in the area. The critics of this alleged Northern policy are generally those who have argued in the past for the establishment of heavy—and generally "dirty"—industrial sectors in Third World countries as an affirmation of economic sovereignty. At any rate, such exportation has yet to take place in the region.

There is considerable consensus among Middle Eastern states on the necessity to stabilize prices of primary exports and to protect themselves from steadily rising prices of imported capital goods and technology. In this vein, several lines of approach are being explored. They include preferential trade agreements, buffer stocks of primary goods, commodity price insurance schemes, and indexing of primary produce market prices in relation to the value of a basket of industrial and technological goods. Indexing is for the moment a major concern mainly of the oil exporters, although the cotton in Egypt, Turkey, and the Sudan; the phosphates in Morocco, Tunisia, and Jordan; and

[60]Sabry Abdullah, "The New World Economic Order and the Struggle for Economic Liberation," p. 79.

eventually the sugar in the Sudan might encourage these countries to advocate indexing. There is, in this respect, some hesitant movement toward the development of international currency reform because of the wide fluctuations in the value of the dollar in recent years. Some have suggested a new international monetary unit of value and a central bank to administer it. Others have focused on the creation of an Arab currency that would be backed by the earnings of the oil exporters. The creation in April 1976 of an Arab Monetary Fund, capitalized at 250 million "Arab dinars" (about $400 million) was a step in this direction. This fund could, in the future, help ease the payments problems of the region's most heavily indebted nations, but it is likely to require "stabilization" programs similar to those of the IMF.

In the short term, there is general accord that Third World voting rights on the boards of governors of the IBRD and the IMF must be increased radically. OPEC countries control only 5 percent of the voting rights in the Bank and the Fund.

Strengths and Weaknesses of OPEC

Let us consider briefly the strengths and weaknesses of OPEC, the world's leading raw materials cartel. OPEC has served not only as the cutting edge of Middle Eastern efforts to redistribute global resources, but also as an example for all Third World countries to emulate. But it is generally agreed that emulation or replication will be no easy matter, for no other raw material as yet rivals petroleum in international trade. In 1974 Northern countries imported raw materials, exclusive of petroleum, worth $40.5 billion, while petroleum imports in the same year were worth $100 billion.[61] The relative stability in oil prices throughout 1975 contrasted sharply with a general decline in world market prices for most other raw materials and primary products, such as copper, phosphates, and cotton. OPEC members have been successful in applying the pricing principle, so forcefully advocated by the Shah, that petroleum prices should be determined

[61]"Le prix du dialogue nord-sud," *Economia*, no. 18, December 1975, p. 13; and Ian Smart, "Uniqueness and Generality," *Daedalus*, vol. 104, no. 4, Fall 1975, pp. 259–282.

largely by the cost of developing substitutes. Other commodities either can be replaced more easily or face greater elasticities in world demand.

Our attention here will be focused on OPEC's Middle Eastern members with respect to this organization's internal cohesion, approach to North-South relations, and performance in aiding regional and extraregional Third World countries. The success of OPEC to date has been based on a minimal consensus among its members regarding pricing and the presumed ability of the North to pay. This is a fundamental point, for it is the common ground for the most pronouncedly accommodationist members (Saudi Arabia, Abu Dhabi, Kuwait) and those who get along with the North out of necessity (Iraq, Libya). In some ways Algeria and Iran find themselves between these two poles, but all OPEC members are convinced, after having been in various ways subjugated by the OECD economies, that those economies are fundamentally resilient and can absorb rising energy costs and remain healthy. In defending OPEC's pricing policies, OPEC analysts have argued, with considerable justification, that OECD stagnation had become manifest well before 1973 and that relative magnitudes in economic power between North and South must be kept in mind. The aggregate GNP of the Arab world in 1974, according to one source, was $125 billion, or 3.8 percent of the aggregate GNP of the noncommunist industrial world. Oil imports represent a transfer to the oil exporters of "a mere 2.6 percent of the combined GNP of the industrial world."[62] In other words, the industrialized nations are economic giants who will find the means to deal with rising costs of oil. There is an undeniable and very important perceptual gap between the Northern states and OPEC in this regard. The OECD North, and most of all the United States, initially treated the

[62]Yusif Sayigh, "Arab Oil Policies: Self-Interest vs. International Responsibility," *Journal of Palestine Studies*, vol. IV, no. 3, Spring 1975, p. 71. See also Boumedienne's speech, March 4, 1975, to the heads of state of OPEC, in Democratic Republic of Algeria, "Mémoire présenté par l'Algérie à la Conférence des Souverains et Chefs d'État des Pays Membres de L'OPEC," Algiers, March 1975; and Hamdani, "Interview with Comrade Adnan Hamdani."

OPEC attitude as confrontationist and hostile, inflicting incalculable damage on an international economic order that, as Henry Kissinger contended, had served the world well. In contrast, OPEC members believe that whatever wounds have been inflicted are superficial and that the rich are not being forced to sacrifice their own prosperity to promote that of the poor.

Having said this, one can then look more closely at the basic lines of cleavage within OPEC, which are ideological and economic. Libya, Iraq, and Algeria are, at least verbally, the nations most concerned about recycling surplus earnings into, first, regional Arab development and, second, the economies of the Third World. The instrumentalities they advocate would be multilateral, run by OPEC, and designed ultimately to break down Southern dependence on the North. The Algerians have proposed a Fund for International Cooperation and Development (a counterproposal to the IBRD's "third window") that would be financed largely by OPEC members at a suggested level of $10 billion to $15 billion. This fund would help finance oil purchases by the oil-poor states of the Third World, offer development assistance on terms similar to those of the International Development Association (IDA), and undertake direct investments. Beneficiaries would have to subscribe to the Action Program of the United Nations for the Establishment of a New World Economic Order, and developed nations would be asked to match assistance in terms of aid, technology transfer, international monetary reforms, and the like. The Algerians have said that if the North responds positively to this "global proposition," OPEC will renounce during a long period any increase in real terms of the price of oil.[63]

This idea has not gone far. First, Algeria and Iraq (whose reaction to this proposal is unclear) would not have to finance the fund; by necessity the responsible states would be those with surplus earnings: Saudi Arabia, Kuwait, the United Arab Emirates, and Libya. But the Saudis are not keen on multilateralism, nor are they likely to be so in the near future, especially when

[63]Republic of Algeria, "Mémoire," p. 103.

120

it is advocated by the area's radicals—nor, of course, is the Shah. Indeed, the Shah has proposed his own scheme of a 10-cents-per-barrel levy that would finance an aid fund. Second, the Algerian proposal calls for a level of financial commitment to which few OPEC members are willing to adhere. As things now stand, OPEC has established a special fund of $800 million to help developing countries ease the payments burden arising from the 1973 price increases. OPEC had originally resolved to pledge $1 billion to this fund, but Indonesia and Ecuador were unable to meet their shares.

Iraq has followed a course unique among OPEC members. It has advocated the complete take-over of all foreign petroleum companies operating within OPEC states and has called for the investment of oil earnings in the Arab world. Yet it was also Iraq that maintained its level of oil production in 1973 when other Arab states agreed to reduce their levels. Iraq has also continued to hold much of its foreign exchange earnings in highly liquid form in Western banks. And at a meeting of Arab foreign ministers in October 1975, while urging an integrated, mandatory plan for Arab development, Iraq let it be known that it does not consider itself a surplus country. Nor does its current development reflect much concern for regional integration. The Iraqi position demonstrates not only the ideological divisions to be found within OPEC but also the economic discrepancies.

Two forms of economic cleavage, each intimately linked to the other, have developed among OPEC members. The first stems from the structural difference between the states with surplus earnings and those that utilize all their earnings for development and military purposes. The latter have an interest not only in high prices but in maximum sales of petroleum to meet their foreign exchange needs. The two goals are not necessarily compatible, but it is really only the surplus-earning states that can afford to cut back production in order to maintain prices. On this question, Iran's interests are similar to those of Iraq and Algeria, whereas on an ideological level they are far closer to those of Saudi Arabia.

The second line of cleavage lies in the pressures brought to bear on common pricing policies by the slackening world demand for petroleum. Demand was reduced only temporarily, and most indicators now point to steady increases in world demand over the next decade. Nonetheless, recurrent recessionary troughs and rising petroleum prices could lead to periodic cutbacks in consumption. In such periods states with ambitious development plans would be under particularly acute strain. They would have to maintain both production and prices. In 1975, attempts to do just that led to open fissures in OPEC's internal consensus. The method generally followed was to offer consumers—i.e., the major international oil companies—covert discounts on petroleum purchases. It may be that Iraq pioneered in this technique, for as total Middle Eastern production fell by about 16 percent in 1975, Iraq's rose 42 percent. It was to compensate partially for cheating by individual member countries as well as to counterbalance inflation in OECD countries that an increase in the price of oil was a foregone conclusion at the September 1975 OPEC meeting.[64] The question then was how much of an increase. Saudi Arabia urged that there be no increase, so as not to further dampen Northern demand, while Iran advocated a 20 percent hike. When Saudi Arabia proved unwilling to alter its position, Jamushid Amouzegar of Iran shouted at Zaki Yamani, "It is intolerable that one country should impose its will on twelve others." To which Yamani replied, "Excellency, my country is simply trying to spare us all the fate of King Midas."[65] OPEC resolutions must be taken unanimously. Algeria, although it probably favored the Iranian position, helped persuade Saudi Arabia to support a 10 percent increase. For its trouble, Algeria was indirectly accused by Iran of an "unnatural alliance" with Saudi Arabia.

In the fall of 1975, discounting allegedly became widespread, although one of the "seven sisters" claims otherwise. Iraq accused the Kuwaitis of undermining OPEC guidelines on per-

[64]James C. Tanner, *Wall Street Journal*, June 27, 1975.

[65]Dia al-Din Baibars, "Petroleum Evenings in Vienna," *Ruz al-Yussef*, no. 2471, October 20, 1975.

missible profit levels for foreign companies (20 to 22 cents per barrel). The accusation stemmed from Kuwait's take-over of 40 percent of the Kuwait Oil Company that remained in the hands of British Petroleum and Gulf Oil. As part of the agreement, the two companies will receive 950,000 barrels a day at a 15-cents-per-barrel discount.[66] Algeria then publicly accused Iraq of similar tactics, while Iran reduced the price on some of its crude oil to encourage foreign companies to increase production and share in development costs of new reserves. This kind of internal bickering is a far cry from the breakup of OPEC which some commentators envisaged a few years ago. In fact, OPEC members in 1976 may earn as much as $112 billion, as compared with $98 billion in 1975. Nonetheless, gradual economic recovery among the OECD countries and the slow development of high-cost alternatives should assure fairly stable prices in real terms in the next decade.[67]

Even if prices remain stable or increase, tensions between collective action on prices and supply, on the one hand, and national needs for development financing, on the other, will continue. Such tensions have been anticipated, again, especially by the Algerians, whose position is that petroleum and petroleum prices cannot be considered in isolation but must be integrated into a program for optimum use of the world's energy patrimony. "[T]he object is by no means to turn a system of utilization and valuation that would lead to one source of energy driving out another but rather to place it in the framework of a management

---

[66]On the take-over, see William D. Smith, *New York Times*, December 2, 1975. For Iraq's attack, see the official government declaration in *Al-Thawra*, November 17, 1975.

[67]A factor working in the same direction is what Franko calls "Catch 24." "Catch 23" is the proposition that if people in consuming societies think oil prices will remain high, they will go down, as people conserve and substitutes become economically attractive. Catch 24 proposes that if oil prices go down, multinational corporations will help push them back up *if* the equity involvement of the multinationals in Middle Eastern industries dependent on cheap local petroleum is massive. Their goal would be to protect their export edge vis-à-vis extraregional competition. Franko, "Industrial Joint Ventures," p. 28.

program suitable for the world's energy patrimony as a whole."[68] Oil, in this view, is destined to be not only a source of energy but, more important, a basic input in increasing food production in the next decades. It is fully expected that as part of this program the North will control its waste of energy and develop new sources. At the same time the Algerians regard current efforts at restraining consumption in the North as a simple power play to try to drive prices down. Such tactics, said the Algerians in 1974, will only oblige OPEC members to cut back production. One wonders if this assurance can be maintained in light of the events of 1976–1977. Saudi Arabia, in a gesture to the new Carter administration, single-handedly imposed only a modest increase in crude petroleum prices by stepping up its production. Other members of OPEC advocated a greater increase but were helpless to assert their view in the face of Saudi production increases.

OPEC has clearly overshadowed in importance the Organization of Arab Petroleum Exporting Countries (OAPEC). Besides the seven Arab members of OPEC, this body, founded in 1968, includes Egypt, Syria, and Bahrain. Its efforts have so far been confined to the promotion of joint Arab ventures, the first of which, in 1973, was the Arab Navigation Company. In April 1974, OAPEC agreed to extend credits to those Arab states most severely affected by the increases in petroleum prices. The total

[68]Republic of Algeria, "Mémoire," pp. 13–14. The United Arab Emirates released figures for their own commitments for aid and grants (actual disbursements are not indicated):

Recipients	1974 ($ million)	1975 ($ million)
Arab Countries	428.2	1,000.0
Africa, Asia	65.0	185.0
International Development Funds	55.2	53.0
Nongovernment Organizations	5.3	5.0
Total	553.7	1,243.0

SOURCE: Figures from Mana' Sa'id al-Atiba, Minister of Petroleum, United Arab Emirates, in "Rich and Poor," *Petroleum* (Egypt), vol. 12, no. 3, September–October 1975, p. 22.

amount of credits extended was $80 million, of which $37.5 million went to the Sudan alone.[69]

In its dealings with the North, OPEC has demonstrated convincingly that if Southern states have a "corner" on a commodity highly valued by the prosperous states, it is possible to alter the terms of trade between rich and poor. But because of OPEC's success, its members find themselves at the very heart of the problem of global redistribution. This position, for many of them, is a dubious honor. As a group they stand accused not only of irresponsibly subverting the advanced economies upon whose livelihood they depend but also of irresponsibly using their ill-gotten gains at the expense of the Third and Fourth Worlds. None of OPEC's members feels particularly abashed by the first charge, but the second touches sensitive nerves. Once again, the situation is that those OPEC members that most vociferously champion Third World causes (Algeria, Iraq) do not, or so they say, have the surplusses to ease the burdens of the oil-less poor. The surplus countries are only beginning to move cautiously into the aid business, but so far predominantly within the region. Iran, with dwindling surplusses, has promoted bilateral aid with a view to consolidating its regional weight, while Libya has recycled some of its surplusses toward political causes (such as Palestinian resistance groups, the Muslims of the Philippines, etc.) as opposed to economic ones.

The performance of OPEC countries, as Tables 3, 4, and 5 show, has been respectable. It should also be noted that developed nations have uniformly failed to approach the norm of allocating 0.7 percent of their GNPs to foreign assistance, whereas in 1974 OPEC states committed 10 percent of their total GNPs to aid and actually disbursed 2.5 percent. To the chagrin of the more radical states, much of the multilateral aid has been disbursed through conventional UN channels or the IBRD and IMF. The special IMF Oil Facility has received over $3 billion

[69]Mauritania was to receive $4.7 million; the Sudan, $37.5 million; Somalia, $7.3 million; South Yemen, $11.3 million; North Yemen, $11 million; Morocco, $8.2 million. Although Egypt has qualified for the IMF special Oil Facility, it was not included among OAPEC beneficiaries.

TABLE 3

OPEC: Aid Commitments and Disbursements, 1970–1974

Year	Commitments ($ million)	Percentage of Total	Disbursed ($ million)	Percentage of total
1970	442.2	2.0	452.1	6
1971	633.6	3.0	635.6	9
1972	580.5	2.7	824.1	12
1973	3,512.7	16.4	1,209.2	17
1974	16,108.0	75.5	3,870.4	15
Total	21,329.0	100.0	7,000.5	59

TABLE 4

OPEC: Bilateral Aid Commitments and Disbursements, 1970–1974

Region	Regional Share of Commitments in % (total: $12.5 billion)	Regional Share of Disbursements in % (total: $4 billion)
Arab countries	75.0	89.0
Africa	3.0	1.4
Asia	18.0	7.0
Latin America	0.9	0.5
Other	2.7	2.3

in OPEC funding.[70] Somewhat plaintively, certain OPEC members point out that the North is demanding a level of performance in recycling surplusses that developed nations never manifested themselves. As an Algerian diplomat put it: "What we are being blamed for is changing the terms of trade abruptly in one commodity and then not instantaneously developing the institutions

[70]In late 1975, Egypt qualified for $50 million in support from the IMF oil facility; it had to raise high-octane-gas prices by 20 percent and undertake other conservation measures to do so.

TABLE 5

OPEC: Multilateral Aid Commitments and Disbursements, 1970–1974

Organizations	Share of Total Commitments in % ($9 billion)	Share of Total Disbursements in % ($2.6 billion)
Arab institution*	15	7.0
Regional institution†	8	0.5
International institutions‡	15	5.0
UN, IBRD, IMF Oil Facility	62	87.0

*E.g., Arab African Development Bank, Arab Fund for Economic and Social Development, OAPEC Petroleum Fund, Arab Investment Bank, Arab Bank for Agricultural and Industrial Development in Africa.

†African Development Bank. Andes Development Corporation, Asian Development Bank, Caribbean Development Bank, Special Fund for Latin American Development.

‡Islamic Development Bank, Islamic Solidarity Fund, OPEC Development Fund.

SOURCE: For all three tables, Republic of Algeria, ''Mémoire.'' Preliminary figures for 1975 show an increase in OPEC aid, with Egypt being the largest single recipient ($1.2 billion), followed by Pakistan ($237 million) and Syria ($198 million). See Mireille Duteil, ''Montée en flèche de l'aide au développement,'' *Jeune afrique*, n. 779, December 12, 1975, pp. 36–37.

to deal with the change. Each change in the Western monetary system has taken around 10 years to implement, and we are being chided for not being much quicker.'' That the Algerian rebuke is justified does not alter the reality that the recycling effort is probably meeting no more than 30 percent of the increased oil burden accruing to the South as a result of price increases. Even the hopes of Arab regional development articulated in the wake of the October War have been to some extent ill-founded.[71]

[71]For a blueprint of what could have been and what yet might be, see Abdullah Tariqi, ''So That the Oil Can Be an Effective Arm,'' *Al-Ahram*, November 3, 1973. Tariqi was a prophet before his time, the virtual founder of OPEC, and a man who long advocated (futilely) a common ''Southern'' strategy on raw materials and dealings with multinational corporations. As an

127

Disposition of OPEC Surplusses

The non-oil-exporting South has been reluctant to accept the moralizing of the OECD North but it has also been reluctant to criticize the redistribution efforts of the oil-rich South. Some Southern nations may see Northern criticisms as an international campaign to divide the South among its constituents. Or they may share, at least vicariously, OPEC's success in turning the tables on the industrial giants of the North—holding out the hope, perhaps, that in the future other nations with other commodities may get their own turn. Despite this reticence, resentment does appear to be building even among Arab states such as Egypt. Black African states, many of which supported the Arabs in the October War by breaking relations with Israel, have received nothing to compensate them for their gesture. There has been discrete and not so discrete grumbling on the part of several African and Asian leaders, including Léopold Senghor and Jomo Kenyatta.[72] At least one Arab voice has sounded the same theme. Hikmat Nashashibi, investment manager of the Arab Fund for Economic and Social Development, has questioned the wisdom of Arab oil-exporting states that keep their surplus earnings in highly liquid form in Western banking institutions. He has also warned certain OPEC states, hard-pressed for foreign exchange to meet their own development needs, against stripping the Eurocurrency markets of funds badly needed by other developing nations. He obviously had Iraq, Iran, and Algeria in mind.[73] For the most part, however, the ranks of the oil-rich and the oil-poor in the Third World have not yet been broken. There is a feeling

active consultant to several Arab governments on petroleum affairs, he may rise to prominence once again in the 1980s. In general, see Stephen Duguid, "A Biographical Approach to the Study of Social Change in the Middle East: Abdullah Tariqi as the New Man," *International Journal of Middle East Studies*, vol. 1, no. 3, July 1970, pp. 195–220.

[72]Thomas Johnson, "Black Africans at UN Question Extent and Motives of Arab Aid," *New York Times*, October 23, 1975; and *Al-Ahram*, December 19, 1975. In March 1977, Arab and African heads of state met in Cairo to discuss the situation. Saudi Arabia and other Gulf states pledged hundreds of millions of dollars to African development.

[73]Johnson, "Black Africans"; and *Egyptian Gazette*, October 13, 1975.

that all the talk of OPEC greed is a Northern ploy to divide the poor among themselves; consequently, poor states, hard hit by rising oil prices, are nonetheless "happy to see those big, bad imperialists in their misery."[74]

OPEC states would like to believe that there is no real conflict of interest, at least not one that is unsusceptible to a fairly rapid solution. They cite the fact that in the Paris meeting on North-South relations the Northern effort (read United States effort) to divide the South into oil- and non-oil-producing states was overcome. This portrayal, it should be noted, does not reflect reality as presented in the Egyptian press, where the non-oil-producing Third World states were referred to as a distinct bloc. The oil producers may in some instances be willing to concede that they have differences with the non-oil producers, but they immediately raise geopolitical points: "[OPEC's] financial contributions to the Third World could be much more substantial than they actually are if a just and durable peace could be established in the Middle East."[75] Their argument is that vast amounts of the earnings of the Arab oil-rich are being siphoned off by the imperatives of confrontation with Israel, i.e., economic and military assistance to Egypt and Syria. It at once shifts the burden of guilt to Israel's Northern backers.

A number of measures are now being considered to strengthen the effectiveness of Middle Eastern OPEC members in handling their surplusses. A first step being taken is the endowment of the region with its own financial and banking institutions and a common, internationally negotiable currency. This will mean an apparent, but perhaps fictitious, gradual decoupling from Northern institutions, which, as Table 6 shows, in 1974 handled nearly $60 billion in oil earnings for all OPEC nations. The movement of surplus earnings to the North has grown since 1974. Exercising collective Arab institutional control over these funds would avoid "the frenzied attempts" of individual states to maximize their earnings in Western markets, ease the strain on reserve curren-

[74]Ray Vicker, "Altruism of the Oil Sheikhs," *Wall Street Journal*, September 8, 1975.
[75]Republic of Algeria, "Mémoire," p. 176.

TABLE 6

Movement of OPEC Earnings to the North, 1974

Deposits in European currencies	$21.0 billion
Deposits in United States currencies	4.0 billion
British deposits and bonds	7.5 billion
United States bonds	6.0 billion
European and Japanese bonds	9.0 billion
Credits to industrial countries	5.5 billion
IBRD/IMF	3.5 billion
United States stocks	1.0 billion
Total	$57.5 billion

SOURCE: Data collected from reports of major Northern banks.

cies (especially the United States dollar), and prepare the way for a rational recycling of funds toward all poor nations—beginning with those in the Middle East itself.[76]

The two great crises of our time—the shortages of energy and food—have stimulated thinking about ways of using oil earnings to help feed nations lacking food. The Third World Forum has called for a collaborative effort between OPEC nations and Third World countries with the potential to produce food. Repayment for financial assistance could be made over time as a portion of agricultural surplusses. The program of the Arab Fund for Economic and Social Development, mentioned earlier, for the Sudan is an initial step in this direction. OPEC will also contribute heavily to the International Fund for Agricultural Development, which is under the auspices of the UN and capitalized at 1 billion SDRs. The Algerians have recommended much more ambitious measures. OPEC, they argue, should undertake joint projects

[76]See Hassan Abbas Zaki (Egyptian financial expert secunded to the Abu Dhabi Fund), "Toward a New Strategy of Arab Investments," *Petroleum*, vol. 12, no. 3, September–October 1975. He also advocates placing Arab funds in the central banks of Council for Mutual Economic Assistance (COMECON) countries. See Sayigh, "Arab Oil Policies," p. 72.

in the production of azote fertilizers in order to meet two-thirds of all Third World needs. Production would be turned over to the UN Food and Agricultural Organization (FAO), which would sell the fertilizers to the neediest at production cost. OPEC would assume freight charges. This suggestion, however, has not gone beyond the stage of general discussion.[77]

Within the Arab world itself a nascent debate, its terms as yet poorly defined, is taking shape. It is one of paramount importance for North-South relations and indeed for all questions of global redistribution, because it goes to the heart of national economic sovereignty. The Sixth Special Session of the UN General Assembly, meeting in April and May 1974, issued a Charter of the Economic Rights and Duties of Nations. It aimed at once at a new world economic order and a ringing endorsement of national sovereignty in all economic matters. Every state, it declared, must have the right to build the economic and social order of its choosing, and its choice should incur no international discrimination. Inherent in this right is *permanent* and *total* national sovereignty over all economic activities and natural resources within any nation's borders. It is hard to interpret this "right" as anything but an obstacle to the new world economic order; it flies in the face of all Third World demands that the North accept the concept of "automaticity" in the transfer of real resources to the South. But the matter comes home to roost with much greater acuity in the Arab world, where the oil-poor states are less and less prepared to accept the sovereign right of the oil-rich to dispose of their resource as they see fit. The debate has not been phrased unambiguously, for even the oil-poor wish to exercise national control over what resources they have, but there is an undeniable sentiment that "the oil belongs to the Arabs" and anything less than sharing the wealth is an intolerable form of usurpation.

In sum, OPEC may well be one of a kind—a cartel widely emulated but not easily duplicated. Until tin, copper, phosphates, coffee, long-staple cotton, and other commodities mean as much

[77]Third World Forum, *Proposals for a New International Economic Order*, Mexico City, August 21–24, 1975, p. 13; and Republic of Algeria, "Mémoire," p. 85.

to the world economy as fossil fuels, new Southern cartels are not likely to arise. Second, to belabor the obvious, we must emphasize that only oil exporters can join OPEC's ranks; it is neither a regional nor a Southern forum or bargaining instrumentality. OPEC's members have pooled their international economic leverage to promote their own national economies, and only secondarily those of other states in the region or in the South as a whole. When OPEC takes stances that impinge upon North-South issues, it does so almost inadvertently and with the national interests of its members foremost in view. Thus, the Shah's repeated call for indexing the international price of oil according to the weighted value of a "basket" of goods imported from the North would benefit only oil exporters. It should also be noted that OPEC is itself internally divided between those states that utilize their earnings almost exclusively for national development plans or military preparedness and those that hold their earnings abroad in liquid form, use them to cultivate clients, or invest them in "hot house" development schemes. The former need every penny they can earn and must therefore maximize their production without driving down world prices. To achieve this requires the cooperation of the latter group, which must neither overproduce nor prove oversolicitous to Northern concerns in setting petroleum prices. Finally, while Middle Eastern OPEC members, with the exception of Algeria, have not taken strong initiatives on North-South issues, they will undoubtedly do so increasingly in the future in order to defuse criticism from less fortunate Southern states. Saudi Arabia's stance in 1977 at the Paris meetings on North-South issues, in which it linked progress in the talks to the price of oil, should be viewed in this light. Its real priorities are revealed by the "secret pact," engineered by former Treasury Secretary William Simon and probably Henry Kissinger as well, by which Saudi Arabia pledged to invest a large proportion of its surplus earnings in United States bonds in exchange for political and economic support. *Newsweek*, which publicized this pact, cited a figure of $17.5 billion for total Saudi placements in the United States at the end of 1976.[78]

[78]"A Mystery Pact?" *Newsweek*, June 27, 1977, p. 13.

Third World Forums

There are, by contrast, peculiarly Southern forums in which the collective political and economic interests of the South can be expressed. For at least three of these forums—the Non-Aligned, the Group of 77,[79] and the OAU—emphasis has generally been upon such political questions as liberation, decolonization, racism, Zionism, and armed resistance. In fact, Arab states have adopted common stances only with relation to political questions concerning the containment of Israel. It has become more common in recent years, however, for these bodies to concern themselves directly with various facets of the new world economic order. One of the most significant meetings was that of the Non-Aligned states in Algiers in September 1973, preceding the October War and the 1973–1974 energy crisis. At this meeting Algeria emerged as one of the Southern leaders, and in the course of the debates virtually all the major questions that were at the heart of the subsequent special sessions of the UN General Assembly, the UNIDO meeting at Lima, and the more recent North-South negotiations in Paris were amply discussed. But in general, Arab states (plus Iran and Turkey) have not established common positions on any of these questions. This is not to say that they have been in conflict with one another; rather, they have perfunctorily gone along with prevailing moods, reflecting at once the low importance of these issues for domestic constituencies and the assumption that the resolutions of these meetings will have no binding effect. UNCTAD, while directly concerned with the economic issues at hand, has done little more than provide an arena in which those issues can be clarified, some bargaining positions developed, and, as at Nairobi, the Northern adversaries confronted. There has so far been no conspicuous Arab or Middle Eastern collective action within UNCTAD.

These forums serve mainly to communicate the intensity with which various causes are espoused and thus to signal to North and South the nature of the real issues and the areas in which compromises might be reached. But one suspects that in the

[79]For a good analysis, see Jon McLin, "The Group of 77," *AUFS Report*, West Europe Series, vol. 11, no. 3, March 1976.

future, as in the present, when bargains are struck with the North they will be concluded within narrower frameworks along the lines of commodity cartels, clusters of states physically proximate to Northern societies, or clusters of other states with peculiar trade links to parts of the North. Such is the case of the 46 African, Caribbean, and Pacific nations that now enjoy preferential trade agreements with the EEC. The Lomé Convention, signed in February 1975, was to provide aid and technical assistance to the signatories and ensure access to European markets for their exports.[80] The Sudan, Mauritania, and Somalia are the only Middle Eastern and/or Arab states among them. Such accords, by extending privileged treatment to one set of Southern countries, constitute yet another instance of the special deal. At the January 1976 meeting of the finance officials of the Group of 77 in Manila, the desire to protect their preferential trade status made the signatories of the Lomé agreement reluctant—but not unwilling—to join the other states in demanding equal treatment for all the South.

A similar sort of special deal may be attainable through the Euro-Arab Dialogue, a series of talks between EEC and the Arabs begun in the wake of the October 1973 War. Predictably, they have been laden from the outset with the politics of the Arab-Israeli confrontation. The starting point was the November 6, 1973, EEC declaration on the October War, which called upon Israel to evacuate the Arab territories it had occupied as a result of the 1967 War. The November declaration was followed by a public recommendation by the French foreign minister that the EEC enter collectively into a dialogue with the Arabs. On March 3, 1974, the Common Market issued a declaration endorsing the notion of direct contacts between the two groups to study possible avenues of joint cooperation, eventually leading to a conference of foreign ministers. A meeting of Arab foreign ministers approved the suggestion on May 20, 1974. Preparatory meetings were held in Cairo in June and in Paris in July with a view toward

[80]The Lomé Convention replaces the Yaoundé Convention that linked 19 African states to the EEC. As of January 1976, the Lomé agreement had not yet come into effect, since only one EEC country (Denmark) and only 31 of 46 non-European signatories had ratified it.

convening, in November 1974, a general committee composed of representatives from all 29 states.

That meeting was postponed at the request of the Arabs in order to allow the Europeans more time to work out their position on Palestinian representation. Matters slowed down considerably. In May 1975, the EEC signed a free-exchange accord with Israel, but in the face of Arab unhappiness the EEC reaffirmed its adherence to the principles of the November 6, 1973, declaration. This permitted the holding of the first serious meetings between the two sides in Cairo in June and in Rome in July. At those meetings the representatives agreed to set up a number of joint technical commissions to study specific programs in economic and cultural exchange.

So far the most important impediments to the Euro-Arab Dialogue had been the Arabs' insistence that political and economic issues be clearly linked and the Europeans' efforts to dissociate them as much as possible. It took some time to find a formula to allow the Dialogue to continue. The sticking point remained Palestinian representation; the compromise was to organize the Abu Dhabi meeting (November 1975) on the basis of two delegations, European and Arab, with no national distinctions among either of them. The Arab delegation included representatives of Palestinian nationality.

The Arabs' political objective was and is to obtain a collective EEC recognition of the PLO and perhaps a direct condemnation of Israeli policies. It is not clear whether there were implications of forcing the Europeans to apply trade sanctions against Israel which would exceed the scope of the activities of the Arab Boycott Office. In any event, the Arabs were unable to move the Europeans beyond the terms of the original November 6, 1973, declaration. On the economic side, the Arabs sought a comprehensive trade, aid, and financing package similar to the Lomé Convention, including the abolition of all EEC duties on Arab industrial and agricultural exports, and devoid of any reciprocal concessions on the part of the Arabs. The Europeans countered that under the EEC Global Mediterranean Policy preferential trade agreements were being negotiated with Morocco, Algeria, and Tunisia, and would soon be started with Egypt, Syria, and

Jordan. Thus, there would be no real need for a replication of the Lomé formula.

Complicating the European position is the "agreement" with the United States not to extend Common Market preferential trade arrangements beyond existing accords or beyond the Mediterranean littoral. The understanding, reached before October 1973, came as a result of United States protests within the General Agreement on Tariffs and Trade (GATT) and other arenas. The EEC stance on the October War merely added fuel to the fire: Secretary of State Kissinger saw the November 6 declaration and subsequent steps toward the Euro-Arab Dialogue as obstacles to his conduct of a Middle East policy. Superficially, however, the EEC would seem unlikely to be able to resist for long the pressures to extend trade preferences beyond the Mediterranean littoral. Leaving aside Saudi Arabia and the Gulf Emirates, whose only exports are and will remain for some time petroleum, Iraq and Iran may bargain their substantial markets for EEC goods in return for preferential status. It is important to note in this respect that the Euro-Arab Dialogue will not discuss energy matters, leaving them to OPEC.

There are three major questions facing the Euro-Arab Dialogue: how to handle the Palestinians and establish a common European policy toward the Arab position on Israel; whether or not to move toward a collective preferential trade agreement rather than bilateral arrangements; and how to counter United States pressure against extensions beyond the Mediterranean littoral. None of these has yet been resolved. Lack of consensus among the European parties to the Dialogue, lack of preparation on the part of the Arabs, and the mix of political and economic objectives have jeopardized the talks from the outset. In many ways these procedural and substantive snags may be prototypical of all North-South encounters.[81] As the energy crisis has waned,

[81]Reginald Dale, *Financial Times*, November 25, 1975; "Dialogue Euro-Arabe," *Jeune afrique*, December 12, 1975; interview with Turim 'Umran, President of the Arab delegation at Abu Dhabi, *Al-Ahram al-Iqtisadi*, January 1, 1976; 'Aliwa Farhāt, "Renewal of the Euro-Arab Dialogue," *Al-Ahram*, November 24, 1975; Zakaria Nil, "This Stage of the Dialogue in Abu Dhabi," *Al-Ahram*, November 28, 1975.

at least temporarily, so has the European enthusiasm for the Dialogue. Still, since the EEC is now and will likely remain dependent upon the Middle East as its major source of petroleum for some time to come, it will have considerable incentive to see that the talks do not fail. As long as the Arabs maintain their focus on political issues and fail to prepare coordinated positions on economic issues, there will be little pressure upon the Northern parties to the Dialogue to make significant economic concessions.

In considering the entire spectrum of instruments, forums, and agencies through which Middle Eastern states could take collective stances on North-South issues, we find that rarely have any of the region's states tried to do so. In the two-tiered arrangement of the contemporary Middle East, the relatively rich have adopted, and will continue to adopt, militant stances on these issues only in order to thwart criticism from the rest of the region and from the South as a whole. The less affluent states of the area, such as Egypt, have refrained from direct and public castigation of the rich ostensibly in the hope that the use of fraternity rather than enmity will coax largesse from Northern nations. Southern states outside the region, however, are beginning to manifest far less patience and tolerance. They are restrained from openly breaking with their privileged Southern brethren by the fear of playing into the divide-and-rule strategies of neoimperialist forces. Finally, the Middle Eastern South may reveal the intensity with which it espouses certain issues through large, unwieldy, global coalitions such as the Group of 77 or the Non-Aligned, but if there are teeth to these espousals, they will be bared only in the more intimate confines of OPEC, the Euro-Arab Dialogue, or the North-South talks in Paris.

FOUR

Conclusion

The Middle East, or at least its Arab portions, has the unenviable distinction among Third World nations of seeing all international affairs through the spectacles of conflict with Israel. This perspective leads to a number of fundamental distortions and assumptions. The Arab states see Israel as the local agent of the North; they believe that if Israel disappeared, so too would many of the obstacles to harmonious relations with the North. Furthermore, they see Israel as a thorn deliberately implanted in the flesh of Arab unity; if it could be cut down to size, Arab unity and the sharing of resources among all states of the region would be within reach. Excessive war expenditures have drained the region. Most Arab governments feel that if ever peace could be achieved, many economic challenges could be managed by drawing on local resources. The rather mechanically repeated assertion that the Arab "nation" constitutes the world's sixth power reinforces the view that difficulties between Arab states and the North are circumstantial, not structural.

Summarizing currents of opinion in this manner obviously entails distortions, mainly through overstatement. Significant bodies of expert opinion throughout the Middle East are well aware that structural problems between North and South must be confronted regardless of the outcome of the Arab-Israeli conflict. Their views have, however, received very little currency among other segments of the elites, not because they are judged to be wrong but because policy priorities lie elsewhere.

By the nature of their social status and career perspectives, Middle Eastern elites are predisposed to pursue accommodationist policies in dealing with the North. Accommodation in this sense means the assumption on the part of Southern actors that their economic aspirations and the economic interests of the North can be reconciled without any of the parties threatening or inflicting irreparable damage upon the other. Accommodationists view the present world economic order as sufficiently flexible to allow the evolution of the new order without entailing aggressive collective action by the South and, more specifically, by its Middle Eastern members. Of course, accommodation may well be attractive to the North only insofar as the alternative would be an intolerable series of confrontations. Thus the possibility of confrontation must be implicit in all negotiating situations. Moreover, because Middle Eastern perceptions of the economic strength of the industrial societies differ sharply at times from those held by the developed countries themselves, an approach that a Middle Eastern diplomat may regard as accommodationist could easily be construed as confrontationist by his Northern counterparts.

Forecasting events in the Middle East has always been a risky proposition, for what happens within limited strata of the region's societies can upend what appear to be the "givens" of any particular situation. Thrusting aside the unforeseen and the unforeseeable, one must still attempt to discern the overall constraints or parameters that will determine the shape and extent of changes in policies or regimes.

First, a unique opportunity may slip away from the states of the region in the next 10 to 15 years. The sudden rise in petroleum prices since 1973 may be seen as a kind of tax on the profligate use of energy in the North (and an unfortunately regressive tax upon the nonprofligate use of petroleum in the oil-less South). A fundamental question, then, is whether the nominal transfer of liquid assets from the North to the Middle East will be used to promote the development of the region as a whole. Northern public and private interests would like to continue to see the bulk of the petrodollars channeled back through their own banks, multinationals, and bond markets so that their economies may continue to prosper despite high energy costs. They would like also to continue to be the chief managers of petrodollar deposits, borrowing long and lending short—frequently to poor countries, such as Egypt, which are starved for foreign exchange. These countries wind up paying more for their energy *and* more for their credit. In other words, one set of Middle Eastern countries has benefited enormously from the energy crisis while another has had, if anything, its position made more difficult. The success of the first group cannot really be judged as a triumph for the South unless the new wealth is put to work for the poor. Yet the odds are that it will not be used for this purpose, at least not to the point necessary to bring about extensive regional growth.

Second, accommodation with the OECD North will be pursued throughout the 1980s by most, if not all, Middle Eastern states. This judgment is based on three assumptions. The first is that the nation-state will retain its primacy at the expense of the pursuit of collective bargaining strategies, thereby perpetuating the relative weakness of individual states in any encounters with the North. A second assumption, possible but unlikely, is that some subregional integration will take place. We have already mentioned the possibility of the emergence of a little "Greater Syria," but other subregions are likely to continue to be marked by internal standoffs. Even if the Fertile Crescent or the Maghreb were to form unified bargaining units, all signs indicate that they would use their strength to extract marginal benefits from the North. Moreover, experience has shown that political animosity to the industrialized nations, contingent largely on the Arab-Israeli dispute, is not incompatible with increasing economic exchange. A third assumption is that Northern reliance on Middle East oil will remain stable or perhaps increase during the 1980s.

Continued dependence will have two effects. It will cement economic relations between the North and those oil-producing states that can absorb a good part of their earnings and want the best technology money can buy regardless of the ideology of the seller—though arms acquisitions *may* be an exception here. It will also reinforce the regional leverage of the Arab states that hold surplus foreign exchange earnings. All of these but Libya are currently allies of the United States. Their "power" is dependent upon their financial capability to cultivate clients among the more militarily powerful but foreign exchange–poor states. That capability will be maintained over the next 15 years, thus consolidating not only the military and technological dependency of certain Arab nations on the North but also the financial and to some extent ideological (conservative Islamic) dependency of the less affluent, densely populated states, such as Egypt, Syria, and the Sudan, on some of the OAPEC states.

For the same reasons that some sort of accommodation with the North is likely, it is possible that some sort of accommodation with Israel, short of full acceptance, may emerge. Yet this modus vivendi will be far more fragile that that with the North, and it will have a much higher probability of breakdown. Continued conflict and hostility with Israel need not, however, undermine accommodation with the North on economic matters. Indeed, United States policy under Kissinger was designed to take maximum advantage of this fact without eroding the status quo in the area. Edward Sheehan summed it up in this manner:

We glimpse here the essence of Kissinger's parallel Middle East policy: for, in fact, this diplomacy has always proceeded on two levels. The first level is the containment of the Arab-Israeli conflict, which he considers almost intractable. The second level is the promotion of American technology, which all of the Arabs (including the radicals) crave and which helps him to buy time whilst he copes with the first problem. In effect, he is saying to the Arabs, "I know what you want—your territory—and I'm working on it. Meanwhile I'll give you *every-thing else* you want to compete in the twentieth century."[82]

A number of developments could totally or partially alter the accommodationist image presented above. For instance, major realignments among states could come about as a result of one or more regime changes in the region. Whether it be a question of a shift in a nominally socialist, secular society, such as Egypt's,

[82]Edward R. F. Sheehan, "How Kissinger Did It: Step by Step in the Middle East," *Foreign Policy*, no. 22, Spring 1976, p. 23.

or of a change from monarchical to republican forms among the oil-rich states such as Saudi Arabia and Abu Dhabi, the challenge to the status quo is most likely to come from religiously motivated reformists within the military. The unstable mix of fierce piety and pragmatic socioeconomic radicalism that may be the wave of the future is currently represented by Muammar al-Qaddafi. No regime is immune to it, and some, such as Egypt, Algeria, and the Sudan, are defensively and preemptively drifting toward it. This threat to the status quo is far more real than anything from the left.

Were regimes of this kind to emerge, one would expect some of the following changes. In economic bargaining, the strategy and tactics of these regimes would be less rational and predictable than those of existing regimes. This would be so for two reasons: first, lack of experience and the implicit rejection of current bargaining tactics (i.e., "rejecting" those who have previously done the bargaining); and, second, an even less clear economic focus than prevails today. The ideological and missionary zealotry of the new elites would be strong, and in quest of the cause bewildering shifts in economic and political alliances would be the norm. Relations with socialist or communist countries would be pursued for purely utilitarian purposes—arms and diplomatic support. Confrontation with the North would manifest itself mainly over political issues—Israel and Palestine—but these could be transformed into full-scale confrontations through the imposition of oil embargoes and the start of trade or monetary warfare. The kinds of direct, violent showdowns that Kissinger and others adumbrated without much cause in 1974–1975 would be more probable if one or two "key" regimes slid or jumped into radical pietism. For that reason, the North, especially the United States, may be on the lookout for Arab Pinochets in order to avoid the advent of more Qaddafis.

At the same time, such regimes would be constrained by at least two factors: They would continue to need technology from the North; and they would continue to rely on their managerial and technocratic elites to implement plans. These elites would be likely to advocate policies in dealing with the North that were more cautious, calculating, and rational than those of the hell-for-leather Muslim reformists. They would also tend to focus more on economic than political issues.

Whether or not regime changes of this kind occur during the next few years, it is highly probable that economic polarization across the region and within individual states will be accentuated. In absolute terms, the oil-rich states will become richer while other states, such as Egypt, may become poorer. Regardless of the resource endowment and ideology of a given state, the gap between rich and poor within each state will widen. Regional and societal cleavages along economic lines can be papered over by the judicious manipulation of patronage and by ideological obfuscation, but within a decade the papering job may well require more paste than these societies can individually or collectively afford. Thus, the 1980s may mark an era of false accommodation and may be followed by one of considerable economic upheaval and growing confrontation with the North. If the North is by that time less dependent than at present on Middle Eastern petroleum, the confrontation may involve interests that are not so vital as they are now. However, inasmuch as the "widening gap" phenomenon is global as well as regional, the confrontation may move beyond questions of energy supply to those of planetary redistribution.

Some would argue that this assessment is unduly pessimistic, but states in the Middle East and elsewhere purportedly following market-based formulas for growth urged by the IBRD or the IMF, or those relying on state-dominated systems, have all performed poorly and have failed to achieve their basic economic goals. There are exceptions—perhaps Iran and Tunisia, possibly others—although "success" has not always entailed increased social equity and more even distribution of wealth, but prudence and precedent would dictate that in the years to come, *under-* rather than *over*-performance is likely.

In sum, the odds seem to be that the financial and military power held by Iran, Saudi Arabia, and Kuwait will be sufficient to maintain the status quo for the next 10 to 15 years. Of course, none of these regimes have firmly implanted institutions nor widely accepted political symbols, and an assassin's bullet could easily although not necessarily change the course of history. Such events are acts of God, ever possible (all Middle Eastern heads of state have been the objects of one or more coups d'état or assassins). Whatever the changes, if any, in governing personnel, the preoccupation, not to say obsession, with national political and economic sovereignty will persist, and middle-class elites will move very cautiously in order not to burn their bridges with the North. Their goal is to promote the prosperity of their peoples without jeopardizing their own well-being, and to achieve it they will need the assistance of the developed countries. Yet even though aid from the countries may be forthcoming, these amounts may be insufficient to extend the accommodation of the 1980s into the 1990s.

Prospects for Economic Growth and
Regional Cooperation

Ragaei El Mallakh

Introduction

The Middle East's significance within the world economy, which became evident only in this decade, will remain undiminished through the 1980s. Since the Industrial Revolution, the economically advanced states now commonly called the "North" have accumulated and continue to accumulate real wealth. Concurrently, they have seen the " gap" between their wealth and that of the Third World, or developing nations of the "South," grow ever wider. Yet since the 1973–1974 increases in world oil prices, the Middle Eastern states that produce and export most of the world's oil find themselves in a unique position between the richer, industrialized countries of the North and the poorer, industrially less-advanced countries of the South. Greatly increased oil revenues, which will continue to grow through the next decade, obviously provide the petroleum-rich but industrially underdeveloped states with a host of new opportunities at both the national and international levels. How they will make use of their newly acquired economic strength is a question of critical importance not only to them but also to other states within the region, and indeed in the rest of the world.

Of the 13 members of the Organization of Petroleum Exporting Countries (OPEC), eight are in the Middle East and North Africa (Algeria, Libya, Saudi Arabia, Kuwait, Qatar, Iran, Iraq, and the United Arab Emirates). They account for approximately 70 percent of the world's proven reserves of crude oil. In the mid-1970s these eight nations, while producing about 40 percent—

or 21,151 million barrels per day (bpd)—of the world's total supply, were supplying Europe with more than 80 percent and Japan with 75 percent of their respective oil imports. And by 1976 they had come to account for over 40 percent of total United States oil imports. Since energy is essential to the vitality of all industrial countries, the Northern nations of the Organization for Economic Cooperation and Development (OECD) have, to a critical degree, become economically interdependent with the Middle East.

While it might be tempting, in an analysis of the Middle East's development prospects and importance in the world economy of the 1980s, to concentrate on the region's oil-rich states and their relations with the North, this would be a mistake. Doing this would give only an incomplete and unrealistic picture, for the development and stability of the oil producers and thus the economies of the OECD nations are affected by economic ties *among* Middle Eastern states. Such countries as Saudi Arabia, Kuwait, Qatar, and the United Arab Emirates are not only dependent on the industrial states for imports of capital goods and transfers of technology, but they also rely heavily on their regional neighbors for labor, cooperation in transporting oil, and consumer goods (particularly foodstuffs). Since, moreover, the same petroleum-producing countries can invest only a portion of the revenues they earn from oil in their own domestic development programs (and thus are said to have "limited absorptive capacities"), some surplus capital is being funneled into investment in the poorer states of the region.

Additionally, the oil-poor Middle Eastern countries themselves (i.e., those that have neither large-scale oil production nor the resultant revenues) have economic ties with the North in areas of trade and transport of quite considerable significance. In Egypt, for example, the closing of the Sumed pipeline (running from Suez City on the Red Sea to the Mediterranean near Alexandria) and the Suez Canal would severely damage the Northern economies. The petroleum "have nots" are of indirect importance to the North as well, because instability in any country can affect other states in the region and possibly jeopardize the security of the North's oil supply. Thus, the concern of governments in the industrial nations with the orderly development of the entire Middle East reflects the common interests of the North and the oil-poor states.

Since the 1973 Middle East war, and in part because of it, there have been four important developments within the Middle East and in relations between the Middle East and states in the rest of the world that will affect both the region's and the world's economies in the 1980s. They include (1) the fourfold increase in the price of crude oil; (2) the reopening of the Suez Canal and resumption of work on attendant logistics and development schemes; (3) the stimulation of economic steps on a regional basis; and (4) the growing realization of the magnitude and significance of trade and exchange of technology between the Middle East and the West. These changes or trends will be discussed in the following chapters.

ONE

Oil and Energy Alternatives in the 1980s

In March 1976 the United States, for the first time in its history, imported more oil than it produced domestically. Moreover, Project Independence, hastily presented to the American public following the 1973 Middle East war, was finally being acknowledged as unrealistic, at least regarding its projected implementation. Even though oil prices at the beginning of 1976 were extremely high in comparison to those prevailing before 1973, they still were not high enough to stimulate commercial development of alternatives to petroleum.

Nor is the development of energy alternatives likely to hurt the Middle East during the next 10 to 15 years. In fact, it will be at least a decade or more before most new technologies can be sufficiently developed for widespread and efficient commercial use. Europe and Japan are relatively long-established importers of Middle Eastern and North African petroleum; their reliance on this source will have to continue. The United States, which became a large-scale importer only recently, is now the world's largest single oil-importing country, and for the next two decades will provide the primary growth market for Middle Eastern oil.

During the first nine months of 1976, United States imports of crude oil rose 30 percent to 5.2 million bpd; the amount from Arab producers climbed more than 91 percent, accounting for 46 percent of total imports. (In 1975 imports from Arab states accounted for 31 percent of total imports.) In fact, the entire increase in United States oil imports was in Arab oil. To put these figures in better perspective, the 2.4 million bpd imported directly from Arab sources equaled 14 percent of total United States oil demand, nearly double the share (7.6 percent) in the same period for 1975. Canada and Venezuela dropped to sixth and ninth place, respectively, among the sources of United States petroleum imports; formerly these countries had been the two largest sources of imports. The major suppliers for the first nine months of 1976 were (1) Saudi Arabia, (2) Nigeria, (3) Indonesia, (4) Algeria, (5) Libya, (6) Canada, (7) Iran, (8) the United Arab Emirates, (9) Venezuela, and (10) Trinidad.[1] Although this trend toward increased dependence on Middle Eastern and North African oil might be somewhat reversed if domestic petroleum production—spurred by deregulation and other incentives—expanded rapidly, by 1990 imports could again increase as production from older fields in the United States began to decline.[2]

The continuing control over prices of oil and natural gas produced in the United States has damped exploration and recovery of domestic petroleum resources as well as development of alternative fossil fuels and renewable energy sources. The most recent forecast of the U.S. Energy Research and Development Administration (ERDA) for the years 1975 to 2000 predicts that the pattern of usage of various energy sources will be largely unchanged. According to the ERDA study, by 1985 there will be little effective use of such sources as geothermal energy, solar energy, and oil shale; the prospects for the year 2000 are hardly more encouraging. ERDA estimates that the United States will continue to rely on expanded output of energy from the current sources of oil, coal, and light-water reactors.[3] Moreover, ERDA warns that coal conversion and increasing supplies of solar and

[1]*Petroleum Intelligence Weekly*, November 8, 1976, p. 9; *Wall Street Journal*, November 8, 1976.

[2]*National Energy Outlook 1976*, U.S. Federal Energy Administration, Washington, D.C., p. xxvii.

[3]Dr. John B. Fallon, Office of the Assistant Administrator for Planning and Analysis, U.S. Energy Research and Development Administration, Washington, D.C., in taped oral remarks to the Third International Conference on United States and World Energy Resources: Priorities and Prospects, University of Colorado, Boulder, Colo., October 19, 1976.

geothermal energy, although technically and economically feasible, would require a significant expansion of these (and related) industries that is unlikely to occur unless encouraged by government pricing and regulatory policies. Similarly, alternatives will not be put forth as long as institutional barriers and policy uncertainty impede them.[4] Among these hindrances are public reaction against the perceived negative impacts of nuclear and shale oil development on the environment and quality of life and the often undefined parameters of government policies on pollution, safety standards, and financial incentives for energy research and development. Faced with this kind of energy scenario, the United States will clearly have a crucial interest in the massive petroleum reserves of the Middle East and North Africa. The extent of this interest was further delineated in November 1976 by the U.S. Secretary of Commerce, Elliot L. Richardson, who estimated that if 50 percent of oil imports to the United States were stopped, the cost would be about $170 billion annually in gross national product (GNP) and some 4.8 million jobs. In 1977, almost 50 percent of the total oil demand was met by imports. With Middle Eastern and North African petroleum supplying possibly half of total United States imports (in both crude and refined forms) by the end of this decade, interruption from these sources could easily produce economic dislocations similar to those described by Richardson.

Although Japanese and Western European dependence (as a percentage of imports) on Middle Eastern oil is greater than that of the United States, in absolute volume the United States is the largest consumer of petroleum imports. For example, in 1975, when demand for petroleum was depressed primarily because of the global recession, the United States consumed 15.4 million bpd of petroleum products (its imports accounted for about 6 million bpd), Western Europe consumed 13.1 million bpd (of which about 10.5 million bpd came from the Middle East and North Africa), and Japan consumed some 4.9 million bpd (approximately 3.7 million bpd coming from the Middle East). Because Japan and Western Europe have never been large-scale

[4]*National Energy Outlook 1976*, p. xxv.

producers of oil themselves—unlike the United States, which until the 1970s was even an exporter—their reliance on Middle Eastern oil will increase only as needed to keep up with economic growth. However, in the United States imports must not only meet increases in demand for oil that result from economic growth but must also fill the gap left by dwindling domestic output. In the cases of Norway, Holland, and the United Kingdom, the North Sea production of oil and natural gas will provide a domestic source of energy that will somewhat reduce the reliance of these states on imports.

Energy consumption remains closely correlated with economic growth. The most recent statistics indicate a resurgence of demand for petroleum, calling for reevaluation of earlier demand projections.[5] OECD states are currently seen as having little chance of reducing their oil imports below the 24 million bpd level of 1974. Further, even with only a modest growth rate (4.2 percent per year), the industrial countries could be importing as much as 33 million bpd by 1985. Assuming a higher growth rate, they might need to import as much as 37 million bpd.[6] In the long range, it is very unlikely that either the demand for oil imports will diminish or the role of the Middle East in the international oil trade will be reduced.

Indeed, Walter J. Levy has argued not only that the much-touted oil "surplus" is nonexistent, but that unless Saudi Arabia raises the production ceiling it set in 1974 of about 8.5 million bpd,[7] there may very well be a shortage before the close of the 1970s. Of the 8.1 million bpd of "spare" OPEC producing capacity as of mid-1976, 3 million was that of Saudi Arabia. An additional 3 to 3.5 million bpd of "excess" OPEC producing capacity was held by Kuwait, Venezuela, and Nigeria, which were hesitant to push production because of conservation policies and technical obstacles. The Levy study concludes that rising OPEC output will be necessary to meet customers' short-

[5] An OECD study, *Energy Prospects to 1985*, vol. 1, Paris, January 1975, already was undergoing revision by an OECD and International Energy Agency committee of experts only nine months after being issued.

[6] *Middle East Economic Digest* (London), August 27, 1976, p. 8.

[7] *Petroleum Intelligence Weekly*, August 23, 1976, pp. 1–2.

term as well as longer-term demands. This scenario does not foresee a drop in crude oil prices; rather, the outlook is for both increasing production and soaring revenues.

Barring any unexpected discoveries or technological break-throughs, sources of energy supply during the 1980s will be significantly influenced by the amount of time required to develop various alternatives to oil. In 1976, the lead time for petroleum was up to 2 years for supply from proven but not producing fields in the Middle East; between 3 and 7 years for United States gas and oil from primary production; and from 5 to 7 years for production in the United States or elsewhere in "frontier" areas now without proven production capacity. The North Sea development was marked by this minimum lead time, while on the Alaskan North Slope there was a 10-year gap between discovery and production. The lead time for nuclear power plants is between 7 and 9 years. Gasification of coal requires from 10 to 15 years. Commercially feasible technology for development of the Canadian tar sands may be available by the late 1970s. If this development is pushed and the government is receptive, the tar sands could become a factor in the Canadian supply scenario by the first half of the 1980s. Finally, extraction of petroleum from United States oil shale would seem to have a lead time even longer than that of the tar sands.

Yet the nature of energy sources in the 1980s will not be determined by lead times alone; rather, it will be influenced by such diverse and knotty problems as the impact of governmental decisions on energy and other raw material trade, the financing of energy development, the kind of environmental and safety standards governments adopt, and the economic ramifications for both producer and consumer economies. For example, the level of oil exports (and that of other strategic, or dwindling, extractive commodities) is not solely a North-South issue. Even among Northern petroleum producers—including Canada, the Soviet Union, and the North Sea nations of Norway, the United Kingdom, and the Netherlands—governmental policies are often nationalistic. This orientation is exemplified by the "Canada first" energy policy announced initially by that country in late 1974. At the time, Canada declared a curb on oil exports to the

United States; the scheduled reduction was for a drop of more than 38,000 bpd to 800,000 bpd by January 1, 1975, to 650,000 bpd by mid-1975, and to zero by 1983.[8] The significance of this Canadian decision is all the more striking because nearly one-fourth of United States crude oil imports have traditionally come from Canada. Yet such an export policy is consistent with the Canadian goal of achieving self-sufficiency by 1980.

One source of oil formerly believed likely to relieve the dependence of industrial nations on OPEC oil is the North Sea. Yet production from the North Sea will actually be quite limited, reaching 2 million bpd by 1978 and a maximum of 4 million bpd by the 1980s. Furthermore, the impact of North Sea oil will be restricted to a small geographical part of Western Europe. And since the North Sea reserves are only 2 percent of the worldwide total, they can contribute only marginally to world supply. Western Europe will continue to depend on energy imports, particularly petroleum. In the mid-1970s, Western European nations were importing approximately 98 percent of the oil they consumed, of which almost 80 percent came from North Africa and the Middle East. Given the estimated demand for oil and the cost of acquiring it from other sources, this dependence is not likely to decline radically in the next decade, nor can the direction of oil trade be altered substantially.[9] For Western Europe, alternative domestic sources to imported oil are limited, at least for the next 10 to 15 years. Coal reserves are being depleted; although coal provided 60 percent of Europe's energy requirements in the 1960s, its contribution plummeted to less than 25 percent by the mid-1970s.[10] Recent European studies as well as the European Economic Community (EEC) Commission's 1974 energy program, which is quite optimistic, envisage reducing Europe's 1985 petroleum requirements by 10 percent. This forecast rests heavily on the assumption that by 1985 nuclear power plants will be providing 17 percent of Europe's needs.[11] How-

[8]*Oil and Gas Journal*, December 30, 1974, p. 23.

[9]Stockholm International Peace and Research Institute, *Oil and Security*, Almqvist and Wiksell International, Stockholm, 1974, and Humanities Press, New York, 1974, p. 75.

[10]Ibid.

[11]*Petroleum Economist* (London), May 1974, pp. 166–169.

ever, expansion of nuclear energy in general has been slowed significantly, especially in the United States, because of rising public concern and growing criticism in the scientific community of both safety standards and the wisdom of heavy investment in the type of commercial nuclear reactors that can now be constructed.

Expanded coal production is an enunciated goal of the United States energy policymakers, but it faces a number of problems. First, coal is not a great bargain. The average price was rising even before the 1973 oil embargo; between 1969 and 1970, it increased 25 percent from $4.99 to $6.00 per ton. Late in 1974, the average price of coal reached an all-time peak, about three times the price before 1969.[12] Second, the use of coal as fuel for electrical power poses substantial environmental dangers because of the high sulfur content of much of the coal mined in the eastern United States. Third, there will be considerable transportation problems involved in using coal, since the best quality (i.e., low-sulfur) coal lies in the West, far from eastern consumption and industrial centers. Fourth, while efficiency and use of coal can be expanded and the resultant pollution decreased through liquefaction and gasification, these processes are very costly and the technologies must be refined if commercial production is to be feasible. An optimistic projection is that by the mid-1980s United States coal production could be more than 1 billion tons per year (the current level being 640 million tons). Synthetic fuels derived from coal are not yet as inexpensive as oil, nor are they expected to be substantially developed until late in the 1980s.[13]

One of the obvious means of lowering the consumption of energy, specifically petroleum, is conservation. However, it might be best to avoid the expectation that this approach will lower demand substantially. Conservation in Europe has nearly

[12]William H. Miernyk, "Regional Economic Consequences of High Energy Prices in the United States," *Journal of Energy and Development*, vol. 2, no. 2, Spring 1976, p. 218.

[13]*National Energy Outlook 1976*, p. 175. During the Third International Conference on United States and World Energy Resources, the consensus was that the unit cost of energy from shale, from geothermal or solar energy, and from other alternatives is about double that for petroleum.

reached its limits, and it was practiced there for a number of years prior to 1973. The high price of petroleum products reduced wasteful consumption. Government-imposed taxes on a barrel of imported crude oil made the European auto owner pay for each gallon of gasoline about half the price of an entire landed barrel of crude oil (1 barrel = 42 gallons of crude oil). For years, European industrial plants have been designed to keep energy costs low. In the 1960s, Americans were paying less than one-third the prices Europeans were paying for gasoline. The critical aspect of energy conservation and policy goals in America was revealed in an April 1976 ERDA report which reversed its earlier optimistic stand on the relatively rapid development of alternatives to petroleum. This view was reinforced a year later by President Carter when conservation was enunciated as a primary objective of his administration's energy policy. The report went on to indicate that alternatives would not be cost-effective before the end of this century. Accordingly, industrial nations, including the United States, will import increasing amounts of oil from the Middle East during the 1980s. And although United States oil imports may not always outpace domestic production, there will inescapably be greater interdependence of producers (the South) and the major importers (the North).

The timing of the first price increase by OPEC, the psychological and economic impact of the embargo by the Organization of Arab Petroleum Exporting Countries (OAPEC), and the worldwide recession all combined to breed several misconceptions. One of these is the notion that the embargo and the subsequent price increase caused financial strains so severe that the world was plunged into runaway inflation and recession. This idea exaggerated and distorted the impact of the OPEC members' actions. Inflation was well under way prior to the oil price hike, influenced by such factors as the impact of spending for the Vietnam War and mismanagement of the money supply in the United States economy, which had a contagious effect on the rest of the world.[14] The funereal predictions of bankruptcy for industrial-

---

[14]It has been calculated that the annual extra cost of imported oil for the United States since the quadrupling of its price until the end of 1975 was about $20 billion, or not more than about 1.4 percent of GNP. For other industrial

ized nations, the collapse of the international monetary system, and take-overs of industrially advanced economies through a flood of petrodollar investment simply did not materialize. Readjustment took place and is continuing to do so.[15]

A second misconception is that the higher oil prices were largely responsible for lower oil consumption through conservation. The reduced demand for petroleum was no more than a very short-term phenomenon traceable to the recession; as the recession eased, consumption of oil rose—as was apparent by early 1976—and the annual growth rate in demand is likely to reach 3.5 percent by 1980 (see Table 1). Table 1 shows that the dependence of the North, particularly the United States, on the Middle East will continue to grow in the next decade at least; this dependence cannot be significantly reduced by Alaskan North Slope and/or North Sea production.

The prophecy often voiced between 1973 and 1976 by pundits in OECD countries, particularly in the United States, was that OPEC's disintegration was forthcoming and would result in lower prices, thus making reliance on OPEC oil more palatable to the Northern consumers. The split that occurred at the De-

---

countries, more dependent on imported oil, the levy was heavier: The 1973 to 1974 jump in the oil import bill was 4.31 percent of Japan's GNP, 2.17 percent for Germany, 3.96 percent for Italy, and 3.73 percent for the United Kingdom. See Gottfried Haberler, "Oil, Inflation, Recession and the International Monetary System," *Journal of Energy and Development*, vol. 1, no. 2, Spring 1976, p. 178. Haberler goes on (p. 179):

How can that conclusion [oil price increase contributed only minimally to United States inflation] be reconciled with the widely held belief that the oil price rise was a major factor in our and in the worldwide inflation? And how can it be squared with the view that the oil price rise was the cause of, or greatly contributed to, the recession?

. . . The oil price rise was not a major factor in bringing on inflation and recession. It was no more the cause . . . than the proverbial last straw that broke the camel's back. . . . it was not the heaviest straw, nor was it the first or last one. If one wants to assign an important role to the oil price rise, it could be done only by stressing *indirect* effects through the reactions of the economy and of government policies.

[15]For an excellent overview of the readjustment processes and rationale, see Hollis Chenery, "Restructuring the World Economy," *Foreign Affairs*, vol. 53, no. 2, January 1975, pp. 242–263.

TABLE 1

Noncommunist World Oil Supply Balance (million bpd)

	1973	1974	1975 (est.)	1980 (est.)	1985 (est.)
United States	10.9	10.5	10.1	11.5	13.8
Crude oil	9.2	8.8	8.4	10.0	12.0
Natural gas liquids	1.7	1.7	1.7	1.5	1.8
Canada	2.1	2.0	1.7	1.8	2.2
Saudi Arabia*	7.3	8.2	7.3	8.5	10.5
Iran	5.9	6.0	5.7	7.0	7.5
Kuwait	2.8	2.3	2.0	2.2	2.2
Iraq	2.0	1.9	2.2	3.0	4.0
Abu Dhabi	1.3	1.4	1.2	1.5	2.0
Algeria	1.1	1.0	1.0	1.4	1.6
Libya	2.2	1.5	1.2	1.5	2.2
Venezuela	3.5	3.1	2.5	2.5	2.5

*Excludes Neutral Zone, which is included in other production.

cember 1976 Doha (Qatar) meeting fueled the hopes of those who are awaiting the demise of OPEC. These hopes might be premature by as much as two decades. OPEC, as an organization with significant clout in international petroleum trade, is here to stay for a number of reasons. (1) The seller's market will continue and be strengthened through the 1970s and 1980s. (2) Both Saudi Arabia and its major price adversaries (the other OPEC members, excluding the United Arab Emirates) realize that their past solidarity within OPEC is responsible for their present power in the oil market and for the increased government take per barrel. Moreover, OPEC was created to *protect* its members against abrupt price declines and fluctuations in revenues such as those experienced in 1959–1960. (3) Although Saudi Arabia may have the technological capability after 1977 to increase production dramatically to meet increases in world demand, it is questionable whether the Saudis see this as a feasible or long-term option. Saudi Arabia would be hard-pressed to justify a

TABLE 1–continued

Noncommunist World Oil Supply Balance (million bpd)

	1973	1974	1975 (est.)	1980 (est.)	1985 (est.)
Nigeria	2.1	2.3	1.9	2.8	3.2
Indonesia	1.3	1.4	1.4	2.0	2.5
Other Far East	0.9	0.9	1.0	1.5	1.8
Mexico	0.6	0.6	0.6	1.0	1.4
North Sea	—	—	0.2	3.5	4.0
Other	4.2	4.5	4.5	5.2	5.5
Total Noncommunist World Production	48.2	47.6	44.5	57.0	66.9
Sino-Soviet bloc exports		1.0	1.0	1.5	2.0
U.S. processing gains	0.4	0.5	0.5	0.5	0.6
Total supply	49.5	49.1	46.0	59.0	69.5
Inventory adjustment†	−1.3	−2.1	1.2	−1.5	−1.5
Total consumption	48.2	47.0	47.2	57.5	68.0
Change	7.1%	−2.5%	0.4%	3.5%‡	3.4%§

†Represents inventory accumulation.
‡Compound annual growth rate in 1974–1980.
§Compound annual growth rate in 1980–1985.
SOURCE: British Petroleum Company, Ltd., *Statistical Review of the World Oil Industry 1974*, London, 1975; William D. Witter, Inc., estimates and calculations as published in Constantine Filakos and Ronald D. Lewison, "Prospects for International Oil Supply and Demand: 1975, 1980, 1985," *Journal of Energy and Development*, Autumn 1975, p. 72.

sustained, substantially higher level of exports, since it already has sufficient capital reserves and has had difficulty using in its own economy the revenues accrued at pre-Doha prices when the production ceiling was 8.5 million bpd. (4) Aside from the possibility that by pumping oil now rather than later (when oil will be scarcer) the OPEC nations are passing up future opportunities for added income, there are political considerations beyond the benefits to be derived by bailing out consuming nations. Many of the fellow OPEC members of Saudi Arabia and the United Arab Emirates are also neighbors, and regional stability is politically desirable. Thus, the pivotal OPEC state of Saudi Arabia must balance its own political position between the OECD and OPEC; unless there are rewards for increased Saudi output—such as real movement in the North-South dialogue through the Conference on International Economic Cooperation (CIEC) and an ongoing initiative and concern, particularly by the United States, in resolving the Middle Eastern political conflict and bringing peace to the region—the regional benefits of lowering production could be more alluring and defensible in Saudi policy-making circles. (5) Within OPEC, one should always bear in mind that the argument is not over whether prices should go up or down, but rather over how much and how quickly they should go up. OPEC's decisions have never been binding on its member governments; this has been a structural strength in that the body only moves on issues of strong mutual interest. Centrifugal forces definitely exist within OPEC, but common interests most likely will continue to bond together the members of the entity at least until the late 1980s.

There is an economic strength and a high degree of policy unity or coordination in OAPEC (and by extension in OPEC because of the key role of the Arab producers in that body), derived not so much from commitment as from a mutuality of economic interests reinforced by other factors. These enhance coexistence if not outright cooperation. There is every reason to assume that material benefits (national participation in or full ownership of production, and movement into related operations such as transport, refining, and petrochemicals) will foster a trend toward conscious producer government commitments to preserving greater coordination in Middle Eastern oil policy through OAPEC and within OPEC.

By chance, those countries with the greatest oil reserves and production capacities (Saudi Arabia, Kuwait, and the United Arab Emirates) are also those whose economies have limited absorptive capacities. They are, therefore, not averse to cutting back production. And, consequently, a conflict over whether to decrease oil output as a means of fetching higher revenues is not likely. That a number of OAPEC producers can cut back output without any curtailment of development or consumption spending wipes away the possibility of a drop in oil prices due to a "production war."[16] As noted earlier, Saudi Arabia remains the key since it lifts the most oil and has the largest petroleum reserves. That country could slash its production by almost two-thirds and still have sufficient funds to meet its development needs; thus it has tremendous flexibility in its output.

Alternatively, Saudi Arabia could raise production to infuse moderation in OPEC price hikes. An example was the 1976 Doha meeting, at which Saudi Arabia and the United Arab Emirates opted for what they considered a reasonable increase (5 percent) after an 18-month price freeze. The remaining 11 OPEC members, as noted earlier, decided on a 10 percent hike to go into effect January 1, 1977. The reasons for the Saudi attitude toward prices and their willingness to raise their production above the 8.5 million bpd ceiling set previously included concern for world economic recovery and a desire to give a political signal that price moderation should be an incentive to the consuming nations, especially the United States, to press for a Middle Eastern peace settlement. By contrast, Iran, with limited oil reserves and higher revenue needs, prefers price increases to expanded production as a means of raising revenues.

In oil policy, Saudi Arabia generally has been coordinating its positions quite closely with Kuwait and the United Arab Emirates. The moderate stance of OPEC on pricing can be traced to these Arab states (as contrasted with Venezuela and Indonesia), whose policy appears to hinge to a large extent on an appraisal of the health of the world economy and possible repercussions on their own potential development resulting from the negative

[16]For a study of projected revenues and revenue requirements of OPEC states, see C. A. Gebelein, "Effect of Conservation on Oil Prices: Analysis of Misconceptions," *Journal of Energy and Development*, vol. 1, no. 1, Autumn 1975, pp. 53–68. Gebelein estimates (p. 65) that by 1980, only Indonesia and Nigeria would have to export the same amount of crude as in 1974 to meet their revenue requirements. States that could decrease production by one-third to one-half of their 1974 levels include Algeria, Ecuador, Iran, and Venezuela; those able to meet revenue needs in 1980 with less than one-half of 1974 output are Kuwait, Libya, Qatar, the United Arab Emirates, and Saudi Arabia.

impact of excessive hikes in petroleum prices. Even the Saudi-Iranian differences in oil policy have been muted by increased consultation and exchange of visits under the new Saudi leadership. Frequent compromises have been achieved on the pricing issue.

Despite their leap into affluence, the oil-producing countries of the Middle East still face two major problems: (1) the inability of development plans in nations such as Saudi Arabia and the Arab states of the Persian Gulf to be realized solely through their relatively abundant capital funds—perhaps the greatest obstacle is that of insufficient labor to execute the plans; (2) the gap between the oil-rich and oil-poor countries of the region.

Affluence in the oil-producing countries has thus far been a stabilizing factor domestically, even in Iraq, which is notorious for political upheavals. Affluence has also been a stabilizing factor regionally; surplus wealth has been transferred to the non-oil states through aid and investment. Although absorptive capacity and revenues will be discussed later in the examination of regionalism, one way of getting some perspective on aid and investment is to recall that for oil-producing countries such as Kuwait, only one-third of the revenues earned by petroleum can be spent at home. The rest must be spent regionally or internationally. In coming years, as the gap between the oil-rich and oil-poor widens, continued stability will depend upon the extent of the movement of economic factors of production (capital and labor primarily) to increase interdependence among the states of the Middle East and to diminish the gap. And because the oil producers have the greatest financial risk, stability in the area is of immediate importance to them. If an awareness of this economic interdependence and of the linkage between stability and a narrowing of the rich-poor gap is not forthcoming on the part of the petroleum-exporting countries, the instances of upheaval could increase markedly in the 1980s.

TWO

The Suez Canal

The reopening of the Suez Canal in 1975 made the Middle East vital to trade again not only between East and West but also between North and South. For almost eight years the closure of the Canal brought economic dislocations, particularly in the movement of petroleum, which is the most valuable single component of world trade. Before 1967, more than 33 percent of Western Europe's oil imports had been shipped through the Canal. During the 1967–1975 closure of that waterway, the United States for the first time joined what might be termed the "major loser" category. Some estimates made in 1971 put the total annual direct cost (including oil and dry cargo) of the Canal closure for noncommunist nations at between $3.4 billion and $4 billion, of which about one-third was borne by the United States alone.[17] India and Pakistan paid an additional 17.5 percent surcharge on non-Canal transport of dry cargo from Northern Europe or the United States; the Arabian/Persian Gulf's surcharge ran at about 25 percent; for nations bordering the Red Sea, the rate was 45 to 50 percent; for East Africa, it was about 15 percent; and for Indonesia, about 10 percent. Moreover, dry cargo moving through the Canal to destinations south and east

[17]Ragaei El Mallakh, "The Suez Canal—Its Economic Significance," in *The Middle East, 1971: The Need to Strengthen the Peace*, Hearings before the Near East Subcommittee of the Committee on Foreign Affairs, House of Representatives, 92d Cong., 1st sess., Washington, D.C., 1971, pp. 341–351; John F. Campbell, in testimony to the Near East Subcommittee, ibid., p. 7.

prior to 1967 accounted for more than 40 percent of all such cargo loadings and unloadings at the Arabian/Persian Gulf ports, 32 percent at Red Sea and East African ports, and 24 percent at the ports of South and Southeast Asia.[18]

While the Canal was not being used, it was somewhat fashionable to relegate the waterway's importance to history—the claim being made that very large crude carriers in international petroleum transport had rendered it largely impractical. This view was extremely shortsighted, taking no cognizance of longer-term economic realities and trends that are likely to prevail well into the next decade. Between June 1975, when the Canal re-opened, and March 31, 1976, more than 9,320 vessels passed through the waterway. Already more than 30 percent of the world tanker fleet is using the Canal. Regional and international assistance has been arranged for improvement of the Canal to accommodate a greater share of the supertanker fleet. In October 1976, an international meeting of the Suez Canal Authority with the World Bank, the Arab Fund for Economic and Social Development (AFESD), the Saudi Development Fund, and the Kuwait Fund for Arab Economic Development (KFAED) was convened to study financing the Canal improvement project.[19] It is expected that by 1980 revenues from the waterway will rise to £E 365 million (about $912 million using the official exchange rate £E1 = $2.50).[20] Technically, the project will enable use of the Canal by fully loaded 150,000-ton and partially loaded 300,000-ton tankers. The anticipated cost is $850 million, an investment in Egypt second only to the Aswan High Dam investment.

Thus, the Suez Canal Authority's plans envisage the accommodation of most of the existing supertanker fleet by the early 1980s. This commitment to improvement of the waterway is premised on several developments anticipated over the next 10 to 15 years. First, the capacity of harbors and facilities at Amer-

[18]*The Economic Effects of the Suez Canal*, UN Conference on Trade and Development Board, Committee on Shipping, 6th sess., doc. no. TD/B/C.4/104, January 26, 1973, pp. 1–21.

[19]*Middle East Economic Digest*, August 13, 1976, pp. 12–13.

[20]*Al-Ahram*, October 22, 1976, in Arabic.

ican ports will mean that crude petroleum from the Arabian/ Persian Gulf producers will have to be delivered in moderate-size tankers. Second, as the major Middle Eastern exporters expand their own refining and oil-related industries, increasing amounts of petroleum will be shipped in refined rather than crude form; tankers to hold these oil products are smaller than the very large crude carriers. Third, in the 1980s more and more liquefied natural gas (LNG) will be shipped northward to the industrial consumers from Iran and the Arab producers. While Algeria began LNG shipments in the 1960s, for the Gulf countries LNG processing and shipment is a relatively new undertaking. Present technology restricts LNG tankers' size to well within the range that can transit the Suez Canal. Additionally, the future of the Canal and its role in North-South economic relations are likely to be influenced by the responsiveness of ship and tanker builders to the specifications of the improved waterway. Then, too, completion of Egypt's Sumed (Suez to Mediterranean) oil pipeline in the beginning of 1977 now further supplements the region's investment in oil movement. The Canal-Sumed combination should soon put Egypt in the forefront of petroleum-transiting nations. This Egyptian role could be enlarged during the 1980s, boosted by production from recent Red Sea petroleum discoveries. Finally, the issue of the waterway's security is becoming somewhat relative: If there is further, or increasing, conflict in southern Africa in the 1980s, even the Cape route might prove less secure than the Suez Canal. The world's stake, as well as the Egyptian and regional interest, in a functioning Canal should expand even more in coming years as the efficiency and security of the Cape route decline and the level of oil and non-oil trade rises.

THREE

Stimulating Regionalism: The 1973 War and Its Aftermath

In the 1980s, with petroleum still a dominant source of energy and with the Middle Eastern producers still the leading supplier to the OECD countries, or North, the Middle East will continue to enjoy a large oil-generated income. Because some nations within the region will have surplus capital while others will bear large deficits, there is likely to be regional diffusion of funds and other economic factors, particularly labor. Most of these countries share a common history and Arabic cultural heritage, and the economic and political stability of one country can and does affect that of others. The 1973 Middle East war and its aftermath proved that, paradoxically, even armed conflict can have positive effects on regional development. Four ramifications of the war appear to be long-lasting and may start a chain reaction, particularly in the economic sphere.

1. The increases in oil prices soon after the October War and the subsequent Arab embargo had a dual impact, the first of which was a near-astronomical rise in revenues for the major petroleum states. These increased petroleum revenues in turn exceeded the capacities of the producers' economies to absorb all the new wealth, which led to a capital surplus. Thus the oil states had to consider where to invest surplus capital externally. For example, Saudi Arabia's ambitious Five-Year Development Plan envisages spending $143 billion during the 1975–1980 span. Yet the dearth of skilled labor, management, and social and economic infrastructure make efficient domestic spending of that

much money almost an impossibility. These constraints have delayed a number of projects and may limit actual domestic spending to about $80 billion, or 40 percent of the five-year funding plan. The regional uses of funds that cannot be spent domestically will have a critical impact on the economies of neighboring nations.

2. The second effect was the spread of the belief among the non-oil Middle Eastern countries—especially Egypt and Syria, which bore the brunt of the 1973 conflict—that the October War was absolutely essential in bringing about conditions conducive to petroleum shortages and a testing of the sellers' market in oil. The near-panic reaction, specifically by some observers in the United States who espoused military action against the Arab oil states involved in the embargo, served to substantiate a growing awareness of the need for regional defense to supplement strictly national defense; in short, the major non-oil-exporting countries, Egypt and Syria, found yet another common ground with the petroleum-rich nations in the Middle East, and vice versa. Even if the Arab-Israeli problem were resolved tomorrow, some common defense policies could linger because of the oil producers' investment in non-oil states and because the major petroleum countries, which have small populations, would benefit from a larger, regional defense pool.

3. The 1973 war caused widespread economic and physical damage to Egypt and Syria, resulting in a reconstruction effort financed by newly developed programs of the oil-rich nations. In early 1976, for instance, what might be termed an Arab "Marshall Plan," spearheaded by Saudi Arabia in conjunction with the Arab Gulf states and headquartered in Riyadh, was created. An institutional focus of this effort is the Gulf Organization for the Development of Egypt, which has an initial capital fund of $2 billion subscribed to by Saudi Arabia, Kuwait, Qatar, and the United Arab Emirates. The Gulf Authority concentrates on financing development projects and Egyptian reconstruction.

4. There are, of course, political elements that can be decisive in the Middle East. In the 1980s, the "superpowers" of the region will be those countries that are characterized by substantial oil revenues, a large population, and the potential for economic diversification and development. Some regional superpowers will

not have all three of these attributes, but will rely on exceptional strength in at least one of them. By these standards, the three pivotal Middle Eastern states will be Iran, Saudi Arabia, and Egypt.[21] Rich in oil and natural gas, Iran also possesses a large population (approximately 35 million) and the agricultural and mineral base necessary to expand industry and thereby foster a relatively balanced economy. It has a sufficient labor force whose entrepreneurial skills are growing. Iran's coastline is the longest and strategically the most important on the Gulf. Saudi Arabia, which has the world's largest petroleum reserves (one-quarter of all reserves in noncommunist countries) and the largest surplus monetary holdings (estimated recently at $45 billion), is a Middle Eastern superpower despite its small population and its unbalanced economic growth. Egypt, which has a population of about 40 million (more than one-third of the Arab world's inhabitants), a strategic eastern Mediterranean location for trade and oil transit, and growing domestic oil production, has the potential to further diversify its economy through expanded industrialization, particularly in petrochemicals, and to draw on its comparatively skilled labor force. Egypt is, as well, the cultural capital of the Arab world. Second-echelon powers would be Iraq, and to a much lesser extent, Syria. The remaining countries could create temporary instabilities, but even a moderate level of cooperation among the three superpowers would enhance overall economic stability and orderly development.

During the 1980s, sustained economic coordination between Saudi Arabia, Egypt, and Iran seems more likely than a situation of rivalry leading to strains or open conflict. In the past two decades or so, and particularly prior to 1973, noncooperation and conflict had negative effects on all parties. For instance, the Yemen conflict, involving Saudi Arabia and Egypt, increased Soviet penetration of the region during the 1960s and also increased Iran's isolation from the mainstream of Middle Eastern politics and economics. It thereby caused bitterness and rivalry

[21]Turkey is excluded from this category because of its predominantly European orientation, which greatly diminishes its regional role despite its Islamic heritage. Among the regional projects with which Turkey is involved is the arrangement for construction of an oil pipeline from Iraq with a Mediterranean terminal at a Turkish port.

between Iran and both Egypt and Saudi Arabia. But the 1973 war set the stage for rapprochement between Iranians and Arabs, which culminated—after much prodding by Egypt—in at least a temporary end to Kurdish hostilities. This turn of events has produced a constructive atmosphere in which the three major Middle Eastern powers seek to cooperate with each other. Many reasons exist for a more cooperative mood. First, it is in the interests of the more conservative regimes of Saudi Arabia and Iran to support economic "deradicalization" of Egypt, which would mean not only moving away from excessive government control in its private sector but also encouraging foreign investment by both public and private enterprises. Second, by drawing closer to Egypt—the largest and most influential of the oil-poor Middle Eastern nations—Saudi Arabia and Iran can deflect much of the hostility directed toward the oil-rich states in the region. Third, both Iran and Saudi Arabia have a tremendous economic stake in minimizing disruptions in the movement of petroleum. They want to avoid repeating the significant supply shortages that resulted in the early 1970s when Tapline (the Aramco pipeline carrying crude oil from Saudi Arabia to the Mediterranean) was temporarily inoperable, Sumed had not yet been completed, and the Suez Canal was blocked. Accordingly, they would like to keep open their shortest transport route through the Suez Canal and use the Sumed pipeline. Fourth, the need, particularly of Saudi Arabia, for both skilled and unskilled labor is likely to further enhance Egyptian-Saudi economic ties. Fifth, Egypt's capital requirements make Saudi Arabia and Iran attractive sources of funds. Sixth, growing investment by both these major oil countries in Egypt increases interest among these three states in maintaining a modicum of cooperation, if only to safeguard that investment. Finally, Saudi and Iranian relations on oil policy have been characterized recently by compromise and consultations, although differences over pricing do exist.

Yet it is difficult to say precisely how much the financial, economic, and population "giants" of the Middle East (Iran, Egypt, and Saudi Arabia) will in fact cooperate. Their recent common efforts thus far have been directed toward achieving a stability in the region which is to their mutual advantage. Each nation, however, will maintain extraregional alignments in pursuit of its global interests. Such nonregional ties may or may not affect the extent of its regional coordination. But whether or not cooperation among Saudi Arabia, Iran, and Egypt leads to the signing of formal treaties, the shared economic interests of the three countries will be conducive to a continuation of close ties, particularly in light of the bitter and expensive lessons taught by the disputes and competition of the 1960s.

For the 1980s, the political rapprochement and tightening of relationships between Iran and Saudi Arabia, Iran and Egypt, and Saudi Arabia and Egypt should have constructive economic consequences regionally, developing the Middle East's prestige and power within the North-South dialogue. Additionally, the landmark agreements between Iraq and Iran, including that ending the Kurdish upheaval in Iraq, should tend to increase regional stability. There have been border settlements or at least a decrease in boundary frictions between Saudi Arabia and the United Arab Emirates. The strengthening of ties between Saudi Arabia and South Yemen would also seem to point to greater political stability.

Obviously rivalries and differences do mar relations among some Arab states, but these should always be kept in perspective. The Syrians and the Egyptians continue to have a tactical discord over the resolution of the Arab-Israeli conflict. This discord has been fed by Soviet policy objectives in the Middle East reflected by U.S.S.R. armaments, political support, and/or economic aid not only to Syria but also to Iraq and Libya. Yet in view of the overall trend toward increased political stability and moderation among Arab states in the region, all parties, especially the North, will find that their interdependence makes it simply too dangerous for them to allow the Arab-Israeli conflict to remain unabated. Aside from the Arab-Israeli problem, the major irritant is posed by the Libyan leadership. Libyan discontent with its regional role is leveled at almost all Arab countries; however, its ability to actively manifest this discontent is dwindling. Libyan oil lost its locational advantage over Gulf crude when the Suez Canal reopened, and Libyan reserves are modest compared to other Middle Eastern sources. Libya's population of only 2 million or so, which is less than one-third of Cairo's inhabitants, limits the country's power still further.

FOUR

Stimulating Regionalism: Institutionalization of Aid-Investment

Having outlined the motives to use oil income for development throughout the region, we must now ask if, and how, these intentions can be translated into action and fact. The 1973–1974 oil price hikes began a major transfer of wealth from the oil-importing to the oil-exporting countries. The North was confronted with problems, but of manageable proportions; the consequences for less-developed nations, in contrast, were sometimes nearly catastrophic, for these states had higher petroleum import bills and suffered from insufficient export receipts and runaway global inflation. In effect, the South was subdivided into the oil-rich and the oil-poor, although the economies even of the OPEC nations are still considered to be "developing." Clearly, the non-oil countries within the Middle East itself—Arab and non-Arab alike—suffered from the oil price increases.

OPEC members responded to this predicament through a number of channels. OPEC assistance disbursements in 1974 alone amounted to more than $7 billion, of which $2 billion was moved through the Oil Facility of the International Monetary Fund (IMF), $2.3 billion through loans to the World Bank and other multilateral development entities, and $3 billion through direct bilateral loans and grants to developing oil-importing nations.[22] The worldwide pressure on the oil producers and the already

[22]Ragaei El Mallakh, "Oil and the OPEC Members," *Current History*, vol. 69, no. 407, July/August 1975, p. 9.

177

existing, if modest, regional aid programs in the Middle East acted as catalysts to expand rapidly both the amount of assistance and the number of extenders and institutions. Only the KFAED, the Abu Dhabi Fund for Arab Economic Development (AD-FAED), and AFESD were established prior to the landmark year of 1973, as shown in Tables 2 and 3.

There are several characteristics common to the performance of the national and regional agencies. First, most loans have been advanced to Arab countries, although since 1973–1974 they have also gone to other developing countries in Africa and Asia. Second, the current paid-in capital of many of these assistance funds is only between one-third and one-half of the authorized capital, indicating the recent inception of the funds. Third, the aid agencies are primarily lenders; since they are designed to maintain themselves with revolving capital, they give few outright grants. Fourth, there is increasing cofinancing among the Middle Eastern institutions and between those agencies and other international bodies that make loans for development. This means that North-South cooperation in supporting projects in developing nations is growing. Finally, the assistance funds try to avoid financial participation in projects that might lead to duplication of efforts or to economic fragmentation in the region. One such undesirable scheme would be a new industry or plant identical to one already successful or established within the same country or in a neighboring state. Similarly, an undertaking involving a river that flows through more than one country ought not to be supported if one nation would benefit illegally or to the detriment of another.

In other words, intraregional Arab assistance by and large is still in the gestation period. Many agencies have only recently been established, and there remains a lag between commitments and disbursements. However, Middle Eastern assistance—like all economic aid generally in the form of loans—is also a form of investment: It upgrades the region's credit-worthiness, enhances its attractiveness to additional investment from other sources (including private Arab oil investors), and bolsters the economic stability of the area. Although often still in its early stages and modest in actual disbursements, this assistance from the oil states can be used as a basis for projections of intraregional aid and investment in the region by the 1980s. The major obstacle to be overcome in funding efficient regional development is the fragmentation caused by so many sources of aid; coordination and even consolidation might prove useful in coming years.

The factors impeding consolidation of the various national funds are those facing most aid-extending countries. They include the desire to maintain sovereignty over the dispersal of financial resources and to retain the use of aid funds as an effective means of supporting or advancing certain political objectives and national policies. Already there are indications of a growing awareness of this problem. In 1976 Saudi Arabia, Qatar, Kuwait, and the United Arab Emirates established the Gulf Organization for the Development of Egypt. Also, the AFESD has expanded its capital and increased its membership. Doubtless, politics will continue to play a role in the extension of aid in the Middle East, as it has worldwide. The political element can be reduced through arrangements in which partnerships of donors, working through international agencies such as the World Bank, would raise the standards of project evaluation and make actual granting of aid more efficient.

An interesting concept aimed at greater stability for Arab currencies and balances of payments has been embodied in the new Arab Monetary Fund, created in April 1976, and generally patterned after the IMF. As the Arab Monetary Fund, which is still in the process of defining its objectives and policies, takes hold, its implications for economic relations between the Middle East and the rest of the world may have a sweeping effect.

Finally, the "whole" of the Arab economies of the region— in terms of their capacity to put oil revenues to use—is greater than the sum of the national parts. This higher regional absorptive capacity can be attributed to (1) regional projects, particularly in transport, communications, regulation of shared rivers, and complementarities in industries and agriculture; and (2) economies of scale to be derived from massive economic enterprises. Over the next 15 years, as oil reserves decline and alternative energy sources appear, if only on the horizon, Middle Eastern

TABLE 2

Arab National Development Aid Institutions: Resources and Operations as of 1976

Institution*	Headquarters and Date Established	Capital-ization ($ million)	Types of Operation	Number and Value of Loans Since Inception ($ million)
KFAED†	Kuwait, Dec. 1961	3,380	Project loans, provision of guarantees, technical assistance	24 $517‡
ADFAED	Abu Dhabi, July 1971	500	Project loans, equity holdings, other forms of aid	27 $279§
SDF	Riyadh, Sept. 1974	2,900	Project loans	6 $330 ¶
IFED	Baghdad, June 1974	169	Project aid, technical assistance	1 $ 10

*KFAED, ADFAED, SDF, IFED stand for Kuwait Fund for Arab Economic Development, Abu Dhabi Fund for Arab Economic Development, Saudi Development Fund, and Iraq Fund for External Development, respectively.

†KFAED also extended grants for technical and feasibility studies totaling $4 million.

‡Non-Arab recipients are Tanzania, Uganda, Rwanda, Sri Lanka, Malaysia, and Bangladesh, which jointly obtained a sum of about $35 million.

§Except for a recent $10 million loan to Bangladesh, the balance was extended to various Arab countries.

180

Terms of Loans and Grant Element (GE)	Sectoral Emphasis	Special Conditions
3–4% interest, 0.5% service charge, generally 10–25 and 4–5 year repayment and grace periods, respectively; GE: 29–48%	Infrastructure, agriculture, industry	The Kuwaiti dinar is the unit of account; loans not to exceed 50% of total project cost or 10% of the Fund's capital; generally, financing is restricted to foreign exchange requirements of projects only; projects must not be in conflict with Kuwaiti or Arab economic interests
3–4.5% interest, 0.5% service charge, generally 11–19 and 2–4 year repayment and grace periods respectively; GE: similar to the KFAED's	Infrastructure, industry, tourism, agriculture	Loans not to exceed 50% of total project cost or 10% of the Fund's capital; generally, financing is restricted to foreign exchange requirements of projects only
n.a.	Infrastructure, agriculture, industry	The Saudi riyal is the unit of account; loans not to exceed 50% of total cost of project or 5% of the Fund's capital; at any time loans advanced to a single country must not exceed 10% of the Fund's capital
n.a.	n.a.	n.a.

¶Some $163 million represent two loans still under consideration.

SOURCES: *Middle East Economic Survey*; Organization for Economic Cooperation and Development, *Flow of Resources from OPEC Members to Developing Countries,* December 6, 1974, and *Addendum* dated April 23, 1975; Kuwait Fund for Arab Economic Development, *Basic Information*, November 1974; Hassan Selim, "Surplus Funds and Regional Development," in Ragaei El Mallakh and Carl McGuire (eds.), *Energy and Development,* International Research Center for Energy and Economic Development, Boulder, Colo., 1974.

TABLE 3

Arab Regional Development Aid Institutions:
Resources and Operations as of 1976

Institution[a]	Headquarters and Date Established	Capitalization ($ million)	Types of Operation
AFESD	Kuwait, May 1968[b]	347	Project loans, technical assistance
IDB	Jiddah (Saudi Arabia) August 1974	910 (may be increased to 2,500)	Participation in equity capital, loans and technical assistance for productive projects in the public and private sectors, undertaking of research and promotion of foreign trade among member countries
ABEDA	Khartoum, Nov. 1973[c]	231	Provision of soft loans for medium and small-sized projects in cooperation with other regional and international lending agencies
AFTAF	Arab League (Cairo) January 1974	25	Loans, technical know-how
AFOAF	ABEDA[e]– March 1974	200	Loans for oil imports
SFANOC	AFESD[f] June 1974	80	Loans for oil imports

Number and Value of Loans Since Inception ($ million)	Terms of Loans and Grant Element (GE)	Sectoral Emphasis
10 $162	4–6% interest; 18–20 and 4–5 year repayment and grace periods, respectively; GE: 25–45%	Industry, infrastructure
Not operational yet	Loans extended must be interest free; equity participation is emphasized	General directly productive activities
n.a.	n.a.	n.a.
n.a.[d]	1% interest, 3-year grace period before repayment	Balance-of-payment support
35 $126	1% interest; 15 and 10 year repayment and grace periods, respectively; GE: 71%	Balance-of-payment support
6 $ 80	Zero interest; repayment over 10 years after an initial 10-year grace period; GE: about 80%	Balance-of-payment support

TABLE 3—Continued
Arab Regional Development Aid Institutions:
Resources and Operations as of 1976

Institution[a]	Special conditions
AFESD	Recipient must be public or private organizations in Arab countries; equity participation by the Fund is prohibited
IDB	Recipient must be a Muslim country or a Muslim community in non-Muslim countries
ABEDA	Recipient must be a non-Arab African nation
AFTAF	Recipient must be a non-Arab African nation
AFOAF	Previous oil import levels as the basis for apportioning of financial assistance among individual states
SFANOC	Previous oil import levels as the basis for apportioning of financial assistance among individual states

ᵃAFESD (Arab Fund for Economic and Social Development), IDB (Islamic Development Bank), ABEDA (Arab Bank for Economic Development in Africa; also called Arab Bank for Industrial and Agricultural Development in Africa), AFTAF (Arab-African Technical Assistance Fund), AFOAF (Arab-African Oil Assistance Fund), SFANOC (Special Fund for Arab Non-Oil Exporting Countries).

ᵇCommenced operation in 1972.

ᶜStatutes approved in February 1974.

ᵈAs of November 1974, five countries were in line to receive assistance: Liberia, Mali, Rwanda, Uganda, and Tanzania.

ᵉThe administration of the allocated funds is entrusted to ABEDA.

ᶠThe administration of the allocated funds is entrusted to AFESD.

SOURCES: *Middle East Economic Survey*; Organization for Economic Cooperation and Development, *Flow of Resources from OPEC Members to Developing Countries*, December 6, 1974, and *Addendum* dated April 23, 1975; United Nations Economic and Social Council, *Multilateral Institutions for Providing Financial and Technical Assistance to Developing Countries*, E/AC. 54/L.75, March 28, 1975.

---

states will have to search for ways to diversify growth—domestic, regional, or international—and thus increase their long-term potential.

Regional development is thus likely to become increasingly compelling for the oil countries. As their oil reserves diminish, the economies of countries such as Kuwait or the United Arab Emirates will be put under severe stress, challenging their survival as separate entities. These states lack an adequate agricultural base, and their small populations and narrow domestic markets make large-scale industrial development economically risky because most industrial output must be export-oriented. It should be recalled that the economic plans of Middle Eastern nations are most often tentative (as with Kuwait and Iraq) or overly ambitious (as with Saudi Arabia).[23] (See Table 4 for provisional data on plans in the 1980s.) Also, there has been a lack of formal and quantified investment policies; aid and investment to date have been characterized by ad hoc decisions, by extraor-

[23]For example, Saudi Arabia's Petromin has announced that the completion date for the massive gas-gathering project has been extended to 1985, with total cost triple that of the original estimate, i.e., $16 billion instead of $5 billion. *Oil and Gas Journal*, November 8, 1976, p. 6.

TABLE 4

Current and Forthcoming Development Plans
($ million)

Country	Expenditure	Duration
Algeria	26,634	1974–1977
Egypt	25,641*	1976–1980
Iran	122,800	1974–1978
Iraq	30,000*	1976–1980
Jordan	2,370	1976–1980
Libya	7,170	1976–1980
Morocco	5,950	1973–1976
Oman	n.a.	1977–1981
Saudi Arabia	143,000	1975–1980
Sudan	n.a.	1977–1982
Syria	19,048*	1976–1980
Tunisia	n.a.	1977–1981
Yemen (People's Democratic Rep.)	218	1974–1979
Yemen (Arab Rep.)	n.a.	1977–1981

*Provisional figures.
SOURCE: *Middle East Economic Digest*, May 28, 1976, p. 5.

dinary extensions in times of crises or other pressures, and by a somewhat unconscious continuation of traditional investment patterns. In the absence of sweeping periodic reassessments, the results have been simply more of the same. An example of investment along traditional lines is the heavy investment made by Kuwait and other Gulf states in 1975 and 1976 in England according to patterns established in the colonial-protectorate years. Especially significant are types of investments, as in hotels which yield returns of 5 percent or less—a poor choice by financial and monetary standards but evidence of a conditioned, psychological bias for investing in "safe," "prestigious," "acceptable" outlets. Once these investment yearnings are sated in the traditional fields of real estate and Levantine trading activities, the Middle Eastern oil countries will still have surplus funds emanating from a nonrenewable asset.

As noted earlier, the flow of capital into the oil states of the Middle East will probably continue unabated through the next decade. Similarly, the economic and political impetus to distribute oil earnings in a way that both enhances regional (and thereby national) stability and helps to achieve economic and financial diversification is likely to remain an important influence on policy. While aid and investment policies and programs will stimulate this process, capital, although one of the factors of production, is not the only factor.

The availability of capital has allowed such countries as Saudi Arabia, Kuwait, the United Arab Emirates, and Qatar to substitute imports for domestic labor, food, and technology in the short term, but the long-term procurement of these three elements remains necessary. Iran and Iraq, which do have populations large enough to enable industrial and agricultural development to be expanded, share with their fellow oil producers a need for technology.

Countries can meet labor requirements by improving the training of their own labor forces and by making working conditions more attractive in order to lure workers from other parts of the region. For example, Saudi Arabia needs approximately 800,000 imported workers for its $143 billion Five-Year Plan. The most logical labor pool is that of Egypt, and the Saudi government recently officially asked Egypt to make qualified workers available.[24] Studies by the Egyptian Ministry of Training and Manpower indicate that the work force in Egypt will increase from 8.9 million in 1970 to 13.9 million by 1985. However, between 1975 and 1985 there will still be covert unemployment of about 2 million. This pool can be used by the sparsely populated oil-rich states in the region on a loan or settlement basis. Other countries have already begun to use Egyptian labor. For example, an Egyptian-Iraqi agreement will export agricultural workers from Egypt to Iraq. Between 1971 and 1976 the number of Egyptians employed in Iraq rose from 5,000 to some 30,000.

[24]*Middle East Economic Digest*, June 18, 1976, pp. 3–8.

Even Iran has moved to establish channels to import Egyptian labor. Of course, there are other Middle Eastern labor pools, including Jordan's and Yemen's, which, although smaller than Egypt's, are attractive to capital-rich, labor-poor neighbors. In 1974, for instance, 22,000 Jordanians left to accept employment elsewhere in the region. Within Saudi Arabia today, almost 1 million of the inhabitants are originally from Yemen.

Acquiring food may be more difficult than finding qualified labor for the Middle Eastern countries. The next 10 to 15 years will be a time of hard decisions concerning food—particularly about the ways in which surplus capital can be used to develop local food sources as efficiently as possible and to secure needed agricultural products from other states in the region. Although Middle Eastern agriculture is not meeting demand, its potential output is substantial, particularly in countries such as the Sudan, Iraq, Egypt, and Syria. While there has been an increase in investment in agriculture—such as the Kuwaiti investment in the Sudan—more is required.

Effective development can result from meshing the need for capital with available funds (see Tables 5, 6-A, 6-B, 7-A, 7-B). If this process is carried out, the Arab world could become self-sufficient in agriculture. Of the 3 billion acres in Arab countries, only 50 million are currently under cultivation, of which 15 million are irrigated. However, it is estimated that an additional 300 million acres are cultivable. Moreover, the economic use of two of the world's major rivers, the Nile and Tigris-Euphrates, could be doubled. It should also be possible to increase productivity: The average output of crops in the Arab countries is less than half that of the world average. The region is now producing only two-thirds (12 million tons) of its grain needs. Yet with greater use of technology and capital, the output of cereals on current acreage could be increased from 2 million to 24 million tons in Iraq alone, from 1.7 million to 7 million tons in Syria, and from 7 million to 17 million tons in Egypt. Similarly, meat production could be almost tripled from 650,000 to 1.6 million tons.

These figures suggest that the Arab world may be able to increase per capita food production despite its expanding pop-

TABLE 5

**Estimates of the Capital Surplus of Major
Arab Oil Exporters,* 1975-1985
(billion 1974 $)**

	1975	1980	1985
Oil revenues†	55.79	55.79	55.79
Payment for nationalized foreign oil interest (−)	1.0	1.0	
Absorptive capacity (−)			
Minimum	12.22	19.6	26.66
Maximum	16.55	32.0	52.10
Surplus capital			
Minimum	38.24	22.79	3.69
Maximum	42.57	35.19	29.13

*Iraq, Kuwait, Qatar, Saudi Arabia, and the United Arab Emirates.

†The oil revenues projections are for the minimum level of revenues, given in real terms (to discount inflation).

SOURCE: Ragaei El Mallakh, Mihssen Kadhim, Barry Poulson, et al., "Implications of Regional Development in the Middle East for United States Trade, Capital Flows, and Balance of Payments," preliminary draft report to the National Science Foundation, Washington, D.C., 1976, chap. 4.

ulation, which could reach approximately 150 million by 1985. If it does indeed manage to cultivate around 300 million acres by that time (admittedly a very high level to achieve), there would be approximately two agricultural acres per person, a density close to that which would then be prevailing in the United States. Development of Arab agriculture ultimately will depend on raising output through mechanization (a capital-intensive process), coordination and specialization among the states of the region, and development of agribusiness complexes. Since those countries with the greatest agricultural potential frequently are not the major petroleum producers and hence, are short of capital, they offer a logical investment outlet for oil-generated surplus funds. But if such development is successful, income from ag-

TABLE 6-A

Capital Requirements of Selected Arab Countries for the Period 1975–1980
(billion 1974 $)

	Capital Requirement (1)	Available Capital (2)	Capital Gap (3)	Percentage of Requirement Available
Egypt	23.47	9.28	14.19	39.5
Sudan	7.21	2.411	4.799	33.4
Morocco	11.02	6.044	4.976	54.8
Tunisia	6.03	5.21	0.82	86.4
Syria	4.6	3.571	1.029	77.6
Lebanon	6.432	3.111	3.321	48.4
Jordan	2.6	1.152	1.448	44.3
Yemen (Arab Rep.)	1.2	0.48	0.72	40.0
Total	62.562	31.259	31.303	50.0

TABLE 6-B

Total Capital Requirements of Selected Arab Countries, 1975–1980
(billion 1974 $)

	Capital Requirement (1)	Available Capital (2)	Capital Gap (3)	Percentage of Requirement Available
1975	8.142	4.341	3.801	53.0
1976	8.92	4.658	4.262	52.0
1977	9.75	4.991	4.759	51.0
1978	10.84	5.346	5.494	49.0
1979	11.89	5.745	6.145	48.0
1980	13.02	6.178	6.842	47.0
Total	62.562	31.259	31.303	50.0

SOURCE: El Mallakh, Kadhim, Poulson, et al., "Implications of Regional Development in the Middle East," chap. 4.

TABLE 7-A

**The Capital Surplus and Its Uses: Assuming High Level
of Regional Cooperation
($ billion)**

	1975	1980	Annual Average 1975–1980
Capital surplus			
Maximum	42.57	35.19	38.9
Minimum	38.24	22.79	30.5
Regional requirements*	5.301	8.342	6.8
Regional debt repatriation (maximum)	1.0	1.0	1.0
Capital flows to developing countries	1.24	1.24	1.24
Residual			
Maximum	35.0	24.6	29.8
Minimum	30.7	12.2	21.5

Regional requirement is defined as the sum of actual flow in 1974 plus additional capital transfer necessary for a 10 percent rate of economic growth in the regional non-oil economies.

riculture in the Arab Middle East would increase from $3.5 billion to about $9.5 billion.[25]

The possibilities for increased cooperation among Middle Eastern states, with subsequent implications for the North–Middle Eastern relationship in the 1980s, are closely linked to the liberalization of large segments of the Middle Eastern economies, which began in the mid-1970s and is gathering momentum. The leader of this movement has been Egypt. In late 1974 and 1975 alone, Egypt concluded major agreements with such corporations as Exxon, Mobil, Shell, Deminex (Germany), Trans-World Pe-

[25]Ragaei El Mallakh, ''Energy Producers and the United States: The Concept of Absorptive Capacity,'' paper presented to the Second Annual Convention of the Eastern Economic Association, Bloomsburg, Pa., April 15, 1976, pp. 4–5.

TABLE 7-B

**The Capital Surplus and Its Uses: Assuming Continuation
of Current Level of Regional Cooperation
($ billion)**

	1975	1980	Annual Average 1975–1980
Capital surplus			
Maximum	42.57	35.19	38.9
Minimum	38.24	22.79	30.5
*Committed capital flows to regional non-oil countries**	1.833	1.833	1.833
*Committed capital flows to developing countries**	1.24	1.24	1.24
Residual			
Maximum	39.5	32.12	35.8
Minimum	35.17	19.72	27.5

*Annual averages.
SOURCE: El Mallakh, Kadhim, Poulson, et al., "Implications of Regional Development in the Middle East," chap. 4.

troleum, and British Petroleum. The government has also changed investment codes to allow for tax exemptions and repatriation of profits. The 1976 termination of the Soviet-Egyptian friendship treaty will probably lead to an even greater degree of economic liberalization.

This trend has resulted in increased cooperation between Egypt and the more economically conservative and traditionally Western-oriented oil countries, such as Saudi Arabia and Iran. Similarly, there is a slower but discernible movement toward liberalization in the economies of Syria and Iraq through expanded trade and ties with the West. The Syrian and Iraqi governments remain politically more closely associated with the Soviet Union and the Eastern bloc than does Egypt. But economic development may change political alignments: Iraq's increasing oil revenues and affluence should do much to reduce its dependence on the Soviet Union. Relatively heavy reconstruction and economic aid has flowed into Syria from such pro-Western and free-enterprise economies as Saudi Arabia, Kuwait, and the United Arab Emirates. Liberalization is likely to proceed even in South Yemen, the most radical regime among the Arab countries, as a result of improving financial conditions. There the revival of economic activity since the reopening of the Suez Canal has centered on port and refining facilities. Again, aid from the oil-rich states has begun to trickle in and is likely to have a moderating impact on the government's policies.

FIVE

The Exchange of Trade and Technology

Within the region as a whole, there is enough capital, land, and labor to sustain development. But those three factors of production can be effective only if accompanied by technology, which is needed by all the Middle Eastern countries, oil "haves" and "have nots" alike. The predominant sources of technology for the future, as they have been during the past century, are the industrial nations of the OECD. Thus, the transfer of technology, with its ramifications for industrialization and improved agriculture, together with the already substantial ties in trade and energy, form the fabric of economic interdependence that links the OECD with the Middle East.

By the mid-1970s, the Arab Middle East had become the fastest-growing economic region in the world. Symptomatic of this growth was the tripling of United States exports to Arab nations between 1973 and 1975, which reached $5.3 billion by mid-decade and is expected to exceed $10 billion before 1980. These statistics alone indicate the large economic stakes not only in the trade relationship itself but in the direction of trade; the United States portion of the Arab market compares favorably with that of the EEC or the Soviet bloc. In coming years, because of higher technology, better product quality control, and patterns of trade already formed, the OECD nations are likely to be the predominant source of capital equipment purchases by Middle Eastern countries.

It is relevant here to draw a connection between the exchange of technology and trade and the education and training of many Middle Easterners in universities and institutions of learning in the economically advanced nations. For in addition to being a form of transfer of technology, the education of Middle Eastern nationals abroad has important implications in trade. Middle Easterners trained in the United States, for example, tend to favor the purchase of goods and services with which they have become familiar—that is, American-produced items. Currently one of every thousand Kuwaitis is studying in the United States. The number of Saudis being educated and trained in the United States has doubled since 1973. And, after years of almost no student exchange, Egyptians are once again coming to the United States. The impact of these exchanges will not be felt until the students return to their native countries and assume positions of responsibility. It is likely that during the 1980s this tie between education and the exchange of technology and trade will be considerably strengthened.

The rates of economic growth anticipated in the Middle East in the 1980s will correspondingly enhance trade. Obviously, high growth rates would require an emphasis on industrial development and greater mechanization of agriculture, and would entail larger import bills. The most important industry likely to be developed in the next decade—and one in which the exchange of trade and technology is particularly apparent—is petrochemicals. Here the OECD countries, and especially the United States, will be much more active partners than the Soviet Union or Eastern bloc because their technology and experience in oil and oil-related industries is far superior to that of the communist industrialized states.

The development of petrochemicals in the Middle East will depend largely on two factors. The first factor is the competitive edge that would be achieved by the production of relatively "mature" petrochemical products, such as ethylene, benzene, styrene, and ethylene oxide. Mature petrochemicals are those for which there is a large volume of demand and a slow growth rate in that demand. The costs of producing them are dominated by raw materials rather than, for example, by labor. Though the required technology is costly, it can be obtained without difficulty. Moreover, unit prices are relatively low, and there is a large volume of highly competitive international trade. Since the oil producers could supply their own crude oil and have more than enough capital to acquire the technology they need, they could produce the mature petrochemical products less expensively than businesses that would first have to buy crude oil from another supplier. Producing less mature products, such as terephthalic acid or polyurethanes, would be less advantageous for the major oil-producing countries, since the process and technology are often more exotic, advanced, and costly than those for the mature product.

The second factor is the likely rise in the low level of domestic and regional consumption of petrochemicals in the Middle East. The Industrial Development Center for Arab States has estimated that as much as 40 percent of the production from new plants will be consumed within the region. Moreover, there will be greater concentration on the production of ammonia and other fertilizers to meet the needs of major agricultural development projects.

Joint ventures involving the transfer of technology from OECD countries to Arab nations will depend on economic incentives, especially the steady supply of required raw materials at a low cost. Assured inexpensive supply is likely to become more important in the next decade or so in light of impending, if gradual, decontrol of United States natural gas prices. Such decontrol, for example, could cause the cost in the United States of ethylene, which is selling now for six to eight cents per pound, to double by 1980. Thus, it could be more advantageous for an American firm to participate in ethylene production in the Middle East. Another incentive for joint ventures is the relatively low cost of energy in the Middle East, which makes energy-intensive production methods feasible. Also spurring participation in such enterprises is the availability of capital itself, especially in the petroleum industry, where the capital-labor ratio is becoming extremely high (ranging from $25,000 to $120,000 for each new job created). Moreover, capital is necessary for the technological advances that can make large-scale plants more efficient and thereby reduce production costs. These larger facilities have increasingly dominated recent construction. For example, investment in plants that produce 50,000 tons of ethylene per year has declined by more than half, while there has been a shift toward investment in plants with a 500,000-ton yearly capacity. The capacity range of new units planned or commissioned during the next decade would require not only the availability of huge sums of capital but also security of supply of low-cost raw materials, both of which are present in the Middle East.

Nonetheless, several obstacles to industrial development will linger during the first half of the next decade. Among the most difficult of these will be a shortage of chemical engineers as well as insufficient labor for plant construction and maintenance. Accessibility of sites selected for plants is important; construction of facilities in remote areas could be 30 to 50 percent more costly than construction in more developed areas. In the case of the projected new industrial complex at Jubail, the costs of providing housing, port facilities, and the like—even if assumed by the Saudi government—will be staggering.

However, the most pressing problem of the near future will be the logistics of the vast petrochemical plants. These logistics— getting materials delivered and moving the products out—include overcoming scheduling problems and enlarging or creating port facilities. Shallow coastal waters, specifically in the Arabian/ Persian Gulf area, have required massive improvement projects to increase port capacity in order to handle a full range of seagoing vessels. Delays in the construction of gas-gathering systems and other difficulties have set back the completion of major ethylene plants in Saudi Arabia and Iran from 1978 to 1982. Of course, these delays will also cause costs to spiral. Accordingly, conservative estimates put the capacity of ethylene production in 1980 at 850,000 tons per year and the output of ammonia at only slightly above 3 million tons. However, if logistical problems are overcome after 1980 and favorable world market conditions prevail, the rate of expansion can be accelerated easily.

Among the major Middle Eastern oil producers in the 1980s, Iran is likely to retain its role as the leading petrochemical processor, if not in the output of a specific chemical at least in its wide range of diversified products. Iran's domestic market is large enough to absorb a substantial part of the most sophisticated petrochemicals produced in the country. Its large agricultural sector consumes much of the fertilizer produced domestically, the rest of which can be exported.

Saudi Arabia, which had very little petrochemical processing in the 1970s, is likely to make significant advances in the 1980s, even though some planned projects are likely to be delayed. (See Table 8 for a brief outline of these plans.) Because the Saudi domestic market is limited, the overwhelming portion of the country's output—like that of Kuwait and the United Arab Emirates—will be for export. Thus the Saudi Arabian petrochemical industry will keep the country heavily involved in trade relationships not only with Northern nations but also with developing countries that require imports of fertilizers and other chemicals.

Egypt is somewhat similar to Iran in that its petrochemical industry has been established longer than that in several of the major Middle Eastern oil-producing states and its domestic market is large, thereby reducing its potential vulnerability to the vagaries of export markets. Much of Egypt's fertilizer output

TABLE 8

Saudi Arabian Petrochemical Projects, 1975–1985

Project	Capacity
*5 petrochemical complexes**	2.5 million tons per year equivalent ethylene
Gas gathering and treatment	1,600 million cubic feet per day
Liquid natural gas line to the West	356 thousand barrels per day
Fertilizer plants†	2 million tons per year

*All but one of these complexes will be in the eastern region, with work beginning on three complexes in the 1975–1980 period.

†Two of which will be initiated in the 1975–1980 period.

SOURCE: Kingdom of Saudi Arabia, Central Planning Organization, *Development Plan*, 1395–1400 [1975–1980], pp. 201–205.

can be used domestically, and expansion of existing synthetic fiber manufacturing appears likely to be profitable. Moreover, a number of recent studies have suggested that the potential for petrochemical industries in Egypt is substantial.[26] By 1980, Egypt is likely to have the highest share (26 percent) of total African investment in petrochemicals, slightly more than that of Algeria and Nigeria (23 and 22 percent, respectively). Of the six North African countries (Morocco, Algeria, Tunisia, Libya, Egypt, the Sudan), Egypt is also expected to be the largest single petrochemical consumer, accounting for nearly half the expected demand for high-tonnage plastics by the early 1980s. Nonetheless, a sizable portion of Egyptian output in petrochemicals still would be for export.[27] In this regard, Egypt's petrochemical industry can benefit from the two major petroleum transit links: the Suez Canal and the Sumed pipeline. Petroleum is expected to play a prominent role in financing Egypt's future imports—through rising domestic production of crude oil and petrochemicals, expanded Suez Canal revenues, and Sumed pipeline profits—along with the traditional receipts from tourism and agricultural exports. Additional financing should come externally through economic assistance and through investment in specific projects aimed at meeting the foreign exchange costs of these projects.

Aside from the petrochemical industry, which is likely to be the single most valuable one in the Middle East in the 1980s, production of iron and steel is also expected to expand significantly—probably enough to meet rising consumption requirements, which are projected to leap from 15 million ingot tons by 1980 to more than 40 million tons by 1985.[28] New technologies, especially the direct reduction process in conjunction with the electric arc furnace, will enable many Middle Eastern nations to enlarge their output. Whether or not the plans for iron and steel expansion can be fully realized in the 1980s, the OECD countries can play an important part either in aiding the actual establishment of the steel industry in the region or in supplying

[26]*The Petrochemical Industry*, UN Industrial Development Organization, New York, 1973, is an example.

[27]Ibid., pp. 20–21, 23.

[28]*Middle East Economic Digest* (London), March 19, 1976, pp. 3–6.

stopgap exports until the regional supply is nearly sufficient to meet demand.

Other industries in the region that can be expanded in the next decade include "agro-industries," such as food processing and packaging, and textile manufacture. Whereas expansion of agro-industries will require large capital investments, the textile industries in Egypt, the Sudan, Syria, and Iraq, being based largely on locally grown cotton, are relatively labor-intensive. Their enlargement would help to reduce unemployment and underemployment.

Heavily dependent on OPEC and particularly Middle Eastern oil, the Northern economies will be confronted by staggering balance-of-payments deficits unless sufficient "recycling" of capital occurs. However, the oil-generated funds of petroleum nations are expected to keep flowing back to the OECD countries through investment and trade channels. Investment is likely to increase not only in the more traditional European outlets but increasingly in the United States. It has been estimated that the cumulative OPEC current account surplus for 1974–1977 will probably reach $165 billion, with net foreign assets by the beginning of 1978 of around $153 billion (about 50 percent of which would be held by Saudi Arabia).[29] Indeed, there have already been some discernible shifts in both the direction and type of OPEC investment. In 1974, 22 percent of total OPEC investment went to the United States; by mid-1976 that figure had doubled. Until recently, more than half of OPEC's investment (66 percent in 1974) had been in bank deposits and treasury bills; in the first half of 1976 only 24 percent went into these outlets. Conversely, the share of total OPEC investment in notes, bonds, and direct loans to the industrialized oil importers moved from 14 percent in 1974 to 30 percent by mid-1976, while equity investment similarly rose from 2 to 9 percent in the same period.[30]

The recycling of oil funds has been shadowed by some psychological fears in OECD nations, and specifically in the United

[29]*World Financial Markets*, Morgan Guaranty Trust Company of New York, September 1976.

[30]*Middle East Economic Survey*, October 11, 1976, p. 8.

201

States, where the specter of a sheikh in Arabia or Kuwait controlling Safeway or General Motors has been raised. Fortunately, calmer minds and realities are beginning to prevail on this issue. In the case of the United States, it should be recalled that foreign direct investment has emanated traditionally from Canada and Europe—almost 60 percent of the total $26.7 billion in foreign direct investment (book value) at the beginning of 1976 came from the United Kingdom, Canada, and the Netherlands; at the same time, OPEC direct investment in the United States was approximately $300 million.[31]

Over the years, foreign portfolio investment in the United States has exceeded direct investment ($36.5 billion as compared with $26.7 billion in 1975), whereas United States investment overseas has been quite the opposite ($133.2 billion in direct and $35.2 billion in portfolio investment during 1975). Moreover, federal law restricts foreign participation in American entities engaged in strategic activities, thereby excluding OPEC investment in some of the areas in which the United States itself has been a heavy investor abroad.[32]

The OPEC states are cautious and conservative in seeking investments; like institutional investors in general, they desire diversified assets.[33] None of the OPEC states "have a desire to acquire and/or control major U.S. companies."[34] For example, Saudi Arabia restricts investment to 5 percent or less of any given foreign firm; it currently owns no more than 1 percent of any firm.

The second form of recycling—trade—will also expand, even

[31]"Foreign Investment in the U.S.," *GIST*, U.S. Department of State, Bureau of Public Affairs, Washington, D.C., PA/MS, September 1976.

[32]Among the restricted areas are atomic energy, hydroelectric power, communications, air transport, coastal and inland water shipping, fishing, development of federally owned lands and mineral resources, and firms involved in classified defense contracts. There are also individual state-imposed restrictions on banking, insurance, and land ownership.

[33]Assistant Secretary of the Treasury Gerald L. Parsky, before the Subcommittee on Foreign Commerce and Tourism, Senate Committee on Commerce, May 3, 1976, cited in Department of the Treasury, *News*, WS-821, p. 12.

[34]Ibid.

though the oil exporters' gluttonous buying spree of 1974 and 1975 is already abating, because of saturated markets and severe logistics problems. Table 9 shows projected imports to petroleum states and other selected Middle Eastern countries, which fall below estimates circulating in early 1975. The OECD will continue to be the dominant source of Middle Eastern imports, largely because it can furnish commodities in demand, such as machinery and transportation equipment, chemicals, manufactured products, foodstuffs, and other items produced through technologically advanced methods. Finally, the transfer of technology, so vital to the goals of industrialization and economic diversification of Middle Eastern nations, will expand the trade ties between the region and the OECD countries.

While huge capital reserves make the oil states of the Middle

TABLE 9

Projected Imports by Selected Middle East Countries*
(million United States $)

Country	1975	1980	1985
Egypt	$5,110.0	$ 6,817.5	$10,983.4
Iran	9,200.0	12,200.0	17,200.0
Iraq	3,700.0	7,400.0	10,700.0
Jordan	357.0	575.0	926.0
Kuwait	1,600.0	2,000.0	2,600.0
Oman	440.0	775.0	1,139.0
Qatar	350.0	400.0	460.0
Saudi Arabia	5,200.0	6,100.0	7,700.0
Syria	776.0	1,140.0	1,836.0
United Arab Emirates	1,230.0	2,000.0	2,600.0

*The projections represent the minimum level of value of imports based on the most severe constraints on absorptive capacity of those countries where applicable.

SOURCE: Calculated from national and international sources and derived from regression analysis conducted by the International Research Center for Energy and Economic Development, University of Colorado, Boulder, Colo.

East in some respects the equals of their Northern partners, they will continue during the 1980s to be members of the South. Consumption habits may be easy to emulate, but the refinement of production ability and techniques is a long and difficult process. Thus, the oil nations can be considered members of the "rich man's club" only superficially; they lack the real wealth of Northern nations, which is measured by long-standing economic development of both human and physical resources. Moreover, although some of the prerequisites to development can be purchased and imported, an administrative structure and tradition can evolve only with time. Thus, even 15 years from now the oil-rich Middle Eastern countries will probably still be less developed than some of the poorer but more established nations in which investment, training, and education for the purpose of development and modernization have been taking place for a century or more.

Since the oil-rich states have their own capital and the region can supply most of the labor they need for development, the North's role in their development will primarily be as a source of technology. Yet OECD investment in the non-oil nations of the area—where capital is needed—will benefit the capital-surplus oil producers, whose economic development and well-being are closely linked to the growth and stability of the region.

In the 1980s the traditional and clear-cut North-South relationship—of the aid-extending North and the recipient South— is likely to become more blurred. Technology will continue to be transferred from the North to the South, but the availability of capital from oil-rich developing states has begun to erode the old distinction between richer industrialized economies and poor industrializing ones, particularly with surplus funds of oil-rich Third World states being invested in the economies of the developed as well as the developing states. This new balance of wealth has introduced a period in which the North and certain Southern states will jointly assist development efforts in the not-so-prosperous developing nations that do not have oil.

SIX

Opportunities and Challenges for the 1980s

During the 1980s the ties between the Middle East and the North will expand and be strengthened as a result of continuing common interests and needs in energy, trade, investment, and technology. Interdependence, after all, is a two-way street, and it perhaps comes closest to bearing equally heavy traffic between the Middle East and the North.

But the Middle Eastern nations—even the oil-exporting states, rich as they are—cannot be classified as developed. Their economies show glaring symptoms of underdevelopment, including unevenness in the degree of development of different sectors, overreliance on a single product—petroleum—and investment bottlenecks. Despite the Middle Eastern oil producers' generally high per capita incomes and balance-of-payments surpluses, their new affluence and impressive rates of economic growth are not synonymous with development; the challenge of the 1980s will be to translate these conditions into development, which implies upgrading not only economic indicators, such as greater sectoral balance and diversification, but also human resources, such as levels of education and health.

The drive for development in the Middle East will not be limited to the oil countries. Other states in the region may be short of capital yet be better suited for balanced growth in agriculture and industry, have older and more durable social and economic institutions, and have enough skilled and unskilled labor to support development if financing could be found—as it can and should from the region's oil states, international agencies, and the traditional OECD sources.

The Middle East should retain its position among the most forceful advocates of a constructive North-South dialogue. Saudi Arabia, for example, has been heavily involved in pushing for the Conference on International Economic Cooperation. The countries of the Middle East, their oil wealth notwithstanding, see themselves definitely as part of the South because of their degree of economic and social development and their political linkages. Development, by its nature and despite extraordinary stimulation, is time-consuming; it cannot be instantaneous nor can it be imported as a prefabricated package. In 1990, the nations of the Middle East will still be rightly classed as "developing," both by economic definition and by their own perceptions. In fact, rapid economic growth is fostering a set of economic problems distinctly its own, including inflation and overheating of the economy and glaring disparities in income and wealth.

Finally, the 1980s should see increased potential for cooperation and coordination within certain Southern regions. This potential should be viewed by the North and in particular by the United States as a positive trend. In this respect, the Middle East may act as a prototype for a regional approach to development because the surge of that approach into international prominence was so obviously based on a concentration of strategically advantageous energy and capital. The impact of regional cooperation in the Middle East could be substantial. It could expand markets, enlarge overall absorptive capacity, produce a better meshing of surplusses and deficits in such factors of production as labor and capital, lead to economies of scale, reduce wasteful duplication in projects, and balance development throughout the region. Regional development could also enhance the prospects for political and economic stability deriving from a higher degree of economic interdependence within the area and a diminution of the gap between oil-rich and oil-poor states. Such consequences of Middle Eastern regionalism would enhance trade, investment, and the transfer of technology, three elements that affect the energy supply, employment levels, and balance of payments of the OECD economies.

Selected Bibliography

Amin, Galal: *The Modernization of Poverty: A Study in the Political Economy of Growth in Nine Arab Countries, 1945–1970*, E. J. Brill, Leiden, 1974.

Annual Review of Energy, vols. 1 and 2, Annual Reviews, Inc., Palo Alto, Calif., 1976, 1977.

Anthony, John Duke (ed.): *The Middle East: Oil, Politics, and Development*, American Enterprise Institute for Public Policy Research, Washington, D.C., 1975.

Aziz, Alphonse, and Mabid al-Jarhi (eds.): *The New International Economic Order and UNCTAD IV*, Institute of National Planning, Cairo, December 1975.

Becker, A. S., Bent Hansen, and Malcolm K. Kerr: *The Economics and Politics of the Middle East*, Elsevier Scientific Publishing Co., New York, 1975.

Campbell, John C.: "Oil Power in the Middle East," *Foreign Affairs*, vol. 56, no. 1, October 1977.

El Mallakh, Ragaei, Mihssen Kadhim, and Barry Poulson: *Capital Investment in the Middle East: The Use of Surplus Funds for Regional Development*, Praeger Publishers, New York, 1977.

Fishlow, A., et al.: *Rich and Poor Nations in the World Economy*, McGraw-Hill for the Council on Foreign Relations, New York, 1978.

"The Oil Crisis in Perspective," *Daedalus*, vol. 104, No. 4, Fall 1975.

Polk, William R.: *The United States and the Arab World*, Harvard University Press, Cambridge, Mass., 1976.

Sherbiny, N. A., and M. A. Tessler: *Arab Oil: Domestic Transformation and International Implications*, Praeger Publishers, New York, 1975.

Udovitch, A. L. (ed.): *The Middle East: Oil, Conflict and Hope*, Lexington Books, Lexington, Mass., 1976.

Index

214

About the Authors

JOHN WATERBURY, as a leading scholar in Arab affairs, ha
traveled widely throughout the Middle East, including sever
long periods of residence in Egypt (1961–1962 and 1971–1977) an
Morocco (1965–1968). Dr. Waterbury received his B.A. in orier
tal studies from Princeton University and his Ph.D. in politic
science from Columbia University. His publications include *Th
Commander of the Faithful, North for the Trade, Patrons an
Clients in Mediterranean Societies* (co-editor), and numerou
articles dealing with politics and society in Egypt and Morocc
At present, Dr. Waterbury is a Fellow at the Centre des Étude
sur les Sociétés Méditerranéennes at the University of Aix-en
Provence.

RAGAEI EL MALLAKH, professor of economics, University of
Colorado, Boulder, is editor of the *Journal of Energy and De
velopment* and director of the International Research Center fo
Energy and Economic Development. He has held grants from th
National Science Foundation, Social Science Research Council,
Harvard University, and Ford and Rockefeller foundations
Specializing in energy, development, and Middle Easter
economics, El Mallakh has written over 80 articles, reviews, an
contributions to such volumes as *Economic Development an
Regional Cooperation: Kuwait* and *Capital Investment in the
Middle East: The Use of Surplus Funds for Regional Develop
ment.*

CATHERINE GWIN is a fellow of the 1980s Project at the Council
on Foreign Relations.